Managing in Complex Environments

Robert S. Atkin
University of Pittsburgh

Kendall Hunt
publishing company

Cover image © Shutterstock Inc.

Kendall Hunt
publishing company

www.kendallhunt.com
Send all inquiries to:
4050 Westmark Drive
Dubuque, IA 52004-1840

Copyright © 2010 by Robert S. Atkin

ISBN 978-0-7575-7793-2

Printed in the United States of America
10 9 8 7 6 5 4 3 2 1

Contents

Foreword

This text has evolved from notes developed over the past 15 years teaching "Managing in Complex Environments," (MCE) the required first course for all business undergraduates in the University of Pittsburgh's College of Business Administration. It is written in outline form with minimal graphics and no pictures, clearly out of today's norms in which seemingly half of a textbook's pages are replete with "action shots" and pretty prose. The result is a relatively brief book with a significantly lower price to the student. As a once reasonably poor student reduced at times, literally, to renting books from others, I am so sensitive to student expenses that I resisted publishing the book until outside circumstances required that I do so. But here it is.

I began the notes because I could not find a text that fit to my design of MCE—what I sought unsuccessfully in the market was a text that was more than a travelogue (if it's Tuesday, let's cover marketing), that reflected but did not dwell obsessively on the formal literature, that had a consistent conceptual framework, that covered topics I believe important, and that was easy for students to use. So, I began to write it. Whether I have achieved all this is for you to decide.

Since the outset, I have covered topics because I believed them important to the beginning business student. At one point, in discussion with a major publisher, I was asked whether the text was an introduction to business or an introduction to management. My response was something like, "Uh, it's a book about decisions made by business people trying to grow their firms successfully." Apparently, that was not the correct answer.

And they were right; the book is idiosyncratic in many ways. I've included things like stakeholder analysis, multiple criteria of firm success, the critical role of interpersonal trust in the marketplace, and supply chain management long before they became hot topics. Although I provide no technical development of either, I have deep respect for the insights of both economic and behavioral views of the goal(s) of the firm and the process of decision-making, and these are reflected in serious (but not technical) discussion. I address topics not usually seen (or seen in any depth) in introductory texts, such as transaction costs, a rather solid discussion of the Porter model, an iterative view of how break-even analysis is used in practice, a discussion of business models, a basic introduction to the capital budgeting problem, and the economic trigger for vertical integration.

I also offer a simple conceptual thesis at the end of chapter two which guides the overall flow of material, namely, that (a) firms attempt to avoid or escape perfect competition in their output markets, (b) firms have basically three avenues to pursue to accomplish this (differentiation, process enhancement, or building new business models), and (c) such avoidance (or escape) requires investment that is inherently risky. While this framework was first posed maybe 15 years ago in the first version of the notes, I think it quite robust in the current reality of business.

Although not a native, I first arrived in Pittsburgh as an Assistant Professor in 1975. I have grown to love this place, and I proudly use many examples drawn from experience with local firms. It was and is a wonderful arena for innovation, invention, entrepreneurship, and sheer will to survive, reinventing itself multiple times since its early days.

Finally, I owe much to many, and to all of them I say thanks. I especially want to salute many, many thousands of students and dozens of TAs with whom I've had the privilege of working. And most especially to *ma chère Monique* to whom I dedicate this book. You're awesome.

RSA Pittsburgh, PA June 23, 2010

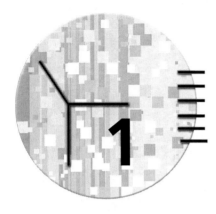

Managing in Complex Environments

I. Teaser.

    A. Maybe this is partly your story. During the summer, you had a job at H & M, better than your previous job at Old Navy. Or perhaps you bought body jewels at Hot Topic, a dress at Juicy Couture, or tickets at stubhub.com. You may have an Acer PC, an Apple iPhone, or returned to T- Mobile for your cell service after a brief fling with Skype. After being unhappy with Hotmail, you now have a gmail account. A world without Twitter, YouTube, or Facebook seems really dull. You vaguely remember a time before SiriusXM. Even though you have eaten more than your share of Wendy's or McD's, and dropped bunches at Starbucks, you've begun to shop at Whole Foods or Trader Joe's. You certainly have watched ESPN or HBO maybe on your family's Phillips giant screen. Maybe you bought someone a gift on eBay or amazon, shopped a bargain on Rue La La, or had a bagel at Bruegger's or dinner at Cheesecake Factory.

    B. What do all of these business entities have in common?

        1. You've heard of them (or most of them – if not, check their websites).

        2. You've familiar with their products (or most of them).

        3. Most are internationally visible and several are not US-based.

        4. Anything else? Your parents are older than most of these companies. In fact, **you** are older than some of these companies. [2]

    C. So what? Really two points:

        1. Business school is not just about getting ready for the job market or graduate school. It is also about getting juiced to create new products, new brands, new jobs, and new companies.

        2. Since somebody will do it, **it may as well be you.**

    D. Hopefully, these notes will be part of a first step.

II. Quick view of two companies.[3]

    A. Many folks still think of Pittsburgh as a smoky steel town even though most of the mills closed decades ago. On the other hand, most folks don't think of it as the home base to newer, growing, interesting firms. But it is – and two of them are Renal Solutions and American Eagle Outfitters.

B. Renal Solutions, headquartered about twenty miles north of Pittsburgh, is a ten-year old firm with a potentially revolutionary home kidney-dialysis system.[4]

1. Although kidney transplant is now a relatively common procedure,[5] renal failure patients may spend years on waiting lists or may not be transplant candidates. Under these conditions, dialysis may be part of the therapeutic regimen. Typically, dialysis requires many hours a week hooked to a machine at a medical facility. It is time consuming, expensive, potentially dangerous, inconvenient, and remarkably destructive of quality of life.

2. After completing FDA clearance in 2005, the firm entered a series of field trials for what the firm calls a patient-centric system. Such systems may provide improved medical outcomes and promote increased quality of life.

3. Challenges faced by the firm range from maintaining high-quality, low-cost manufacture in compliance with regulatory and medical protocol to finding and keeping excellent employees to working with clients who have life threatening disease to fending off competitive pressures.

4. Their continued success requires that they know well how to manage in complex environments.

5. You can check out the company at http://www.renalsolutionsinc.com.

C. Most of you own something from American Eagle Outfitters. Begun in the late 1970s and now headquartered on Pittsburgh's South Side, it is a designer and retailer of casual clothes for teens, college kids, and young adults.

1. American Eagle didn't always have its current focus. It began (as its name suggests) as a provider of camping and outdoors clothing and accessories. By the late 1980s, however, business was flat, so in 1992 they refocused the firm – first, to women, to informal clothing, and to a younger target market. Risky shift, but it seems to have been successful. Since then, they added men's casual, expanded, and emerged as a serious player in the fierce competition for a retail apparel buck.

2. Retail, and in particular retail focused on younger markets, is extremely competitive. Continued success requires that American Eagle understands well not just "kid-fashion," but also such mundane things as cost control, distribution, merchandising, advertising, etc. (See www.ae.com.)

3. Again, expertise in managing in complex environments is critical.

D. What makes environments complex?

1. While these two firms are vastly different, they both face similar general problems. For example (in no particular order) . . .

   a. Product *demand* is difficult to predict. Simply providing the correct amount of product in an efficient and timely manner is difficult.

   b. *Customer needs* keep changing. Just keeping up with the changing needs of existing customers (and finding new customers) is difficult.

   c. Critical *underlying technologies* are complex and keep changing. Just maintaining a technology edge is difficult.

   d. *New products* constantly enter the market, often with short lifetimes. Designing and introducing new products is risky and difficult.

   e. Firms require money. Competition for the necessary financing is fierce, and maintaining a competitive stance in the *capital market* is difficult, especially in today's credit starved economy.

   f. A *talented work force* is required. Finding and recruiting these folks, getting them to join and stay with the firm, and motivating them is difficult.

   g. *Competition* is awesome, producing aggressive battle among current players for industry leadership.

   h. *New players*, with alternative products and ways of doing business, may enter the industry, and increasingly they can be located anywhere in the world.

   i. Federal and local *regulations* affect all firms. Monitoring them, responding to them, and trying to influence them is difficult.

   j. New technologies and new products are often incompatible with existing products and services. Being able to superimpose *technical standards* usually yields great advantages to the successful firm.

    k. *Managing supply chains* so that the firm has the right amount of raw material and finished good at the right time in the right place given global sourcing and multiple distributions points is remarkably difficult to accomplish effectively and efficiently.

    l. Given the corporate debacles of the past few years, earning and keeping public *credibility* is critical and difficult.

    m. Although redundant with some of the above, business today is *global*, producing both opportunity and threat.

    n. Finally, anticipating and reacting to *changing economic conditions* is difficult.

2. Another way of saying all this is to observe the following. . .

    a. The future is not exactly predictable and significant random events do occur.

    b. Therefore, firms must <u>continuously estimate many different critical future conditions</u> (from buyer acceptance of a new product, to the number of employees needed next month, to interest rates, to changes in law or regulation, and so on).

    c. Some of these estimates are short term (days or weeks) and others are longer term (seasons or years).

    d. Estimates are always subject to error, and errors could be massive.

    e. Based on these estimates, firms must make decisions today. Once "done," these decisions may be difficult or impossible to "undo."

    f. Usually these decisions involve investments – that is, the long-term commitment of resources such as time and money. Such investments are always risky, exactly because estimation of the future always has error.

    g. The more complex the environment, the more likely the estimates are incorrect, the more likely investments are inappropriate or flat out wrong, and the more likely the firm will not be successful or in fact fail.

3. We have just completed a year plus run in which this sequence was painfully evident,[6] and we have seen a huge number of business failures among firms that a few years ago were industry leaders.[7] Or more bluntly, past success, even over decades, does not tell us much about the future.

E. So what?

> 1. To be successful, firms must <u>simultaneously</u> attend to, anticipate, understand, respond to, and lead developments in many areas, each one of which is difficult to do.

2. Doing all this, <u>while</u> efficiently using resources <u>and</u> making a profit <u>and</u> being a decent corporate citizen <u>and</u> operating within the law, is an example of what we mean by "**managing in complex environments**."

3. A more extensive discussion follows. But first we need to distinguish the firm from its environment and introduce a few basic terms.

III. Organizations, firms, and environments.

A. Organizations have four distinguishing features:

1. They are **social inventions** consisting of people and other resources.

2. They have a more or less discernable **external boundary** that separates them from everything else in the world and usually many **internal** boundaries that separate various units of the organization.

3. They have **goals** that they attempt to accomplish.

    a. In economics courses, we usually assume that business organizations have one goal: wealth maximization for their owners.[8]

    b. Later in this note, we address whether a "one goal" model captures well the choices made by modern business organizations.

    c. Suffice for now is that organizations have a least one goal, and generally more.

4. They have **deliberately structured tasks**. That is, usually everyone in the organization does different things, and the allocation of tasks to people usually isn't random.

    a. A **position** is a particular set of deliberately structured tasks – business organizations hire (or promote) people to fill positions.

    b. Put a person in a position and we have a **job** – people do jobs.

B. In this course, our interest is with a subset of organizations called firms.
  1. In general terms, firms are either **for-profit** or **not-for-profit**.
  2. In this course, we are interested only in for-profit firms (I use the term firm for the rest of these notes to refer to for-profit firms).[9]
C. Firms have all the features of an organization plus a few more.
  1. Firms have a **legal existence and identity**.[10]
  2. Firms have certain **rights and obligations** determined by legal and other bases.[11]
  3. Firms have some level of concern with the **creation of economic wealth** to provide benefit to their owners.[12]

D. Everything not within the firm's boundary is in its environment.

  1. The distinction may sound simple, but it isn't.
    a. For example, firms have employees. But these same employees are also consumers, parents, voters, and so on, and as such, are also in the environment.
    b. As factors in the environment, they are consumers with varying buying habits; parents with differing views on what's good for their families; voters with differing political goals; believers with different moral, ethical, and religious views; and so on.
    c. Indeed, exactly what's inside the boundary of a firm is sometimes clear but often isn't.
    d. Moreover, exactly how a firm can or should deploy elements within its legal borders is often the subject of much interest among those both inside and outside the firm. For example . . .
      (1) Stockholders (who are the owners of the firm if the firm is a corporation) can and do bring suit against the firms in which they hold stock to protest certain decisions by the firm's management (often called a shareholder action).
      (2) Employees can and do withhold labor (a strike).
      (3) Consumers can and do boycott the products of a firm (a product boycott).
    e. These actions are, though not that common, more or less normal. On the other hand, the recent revelations of apparently massive impropriety by some firms are certainly dramatic, but probably not normal.
    f. These actions can also cause CEOs (and other managers) to lose their job, such as the removal of Mr. Nardelli at Home Depot, Mr. O'Neill from Merrill Lynch, and Mr. Prince from Citibank, even before the recent market collapse.[13]
  2. We assume that firms must interact with their environments to survive and thrive. That is, firms are not closed systems. We call this assumption the **open system hypothesis**.
    a. We call these interactions **transactions**.
    b. Much of what occurs in the environment affects the firm, and much of what the firm does affects its environment. For a current example, the collapse of Lehman Brothers, a major investment bank, contributed big time to the freeze-up in the global credit markets a year ago.
    c. The open systems hypothesis requires that we view the firm and its environment as a single dynamic system, even though we can and will treat the firm and the environment as separate entities.
  3. Please note that a firm's environment contains all other firms. Hence, the environment of each firm is unique (as an exercise, please "prove" this to yourself).

IV. So given all this, what is a "complex environment"?

  A. A complex environment is one marked by rapid, large scale, and uncertain change in many underlying business drivers each with a different set of dynamics.

    1. So, we need to address **change** and **drivers**.
    2. And as we see below, each has several components.
  B. Change.
    1. **Rate of change**.
      a. Today, the environment of many, perhaps most businesses, is changing rapidly.

b. Think about CPUs, the "brain" of your PC. From 1982 to 2002, Intel introduced the following CPUs for PC use: the 8088, 8086, 286, 386, 486 (small version), 486 (more powerful versions), Pentium®, Pentium® with MMX™, Pentium II®, Pentium III®, and Pentium 4®. Perhaps eleven generations in about twenty years! And many more since then.

c. Imagine you are Dell, a PC maker. Intel is "in" your environment, and each new chip generation seriously changes that environment. If you don't quickly introduce new PCs using the new chip's potential, your business may quickly suffer, as others will exploit this potential.[14]

d. During this time, the buyer's price per unit of computing power dropped rapidly. For example, my 1995 Toshiba Satellite Pro™ T2150CDS laptop cost about $3300. While not top of the line, it was impressive for its day: 10" dual scan color screen, 75 MHZ 486 CPU, 8 megs of RAM, a 520 meg hard drive, and 4× CD. But by today's standards, it's nearly useless. Couldn't really connect to the Internet. Awful sound. SLOW. No DVD or wireless. Finally, really expensive compared to what I can get today for a third the price.[15]

e. Not only has price per computing unit dropped, but also the time between each of these generations has shrunk. (Think how quickly your mobile phone goes from slick and hot to old hat.)

f. While rates of change vary across industries, and change isn't always this rapid, things move even more quickly in many environments.[16]

g. My point: **The faster the rate of change, the more complex the environment**.

2. **Magnitude of change**. The sheer size of the change is often very large.

a. Today, the Internet seems everywhere, yet a decade ago it was simply an arcane curiosity of little interest to most people.

b. Today, we all know Google – its founders didn't meet each other until 1995. No eBay, no downloadable music, etc. when you were born.[17]

c. But it's not just technology that affects the size of change. For example, during the recent recession, more than 10 million jobs in the United States evaporated.

d. **The greater the magnitude of change, the more complex the environment**.

3. **Uncertainty of change**. If rapid or large-scale change were easily predictable by firms, then anticipating and responding to it would not that difficult. However, change itself is difficult to predict. The sources of change keep changing, making the uncertainty of change a major issue.

a. Some time ago, for example, Bill Gates admitted (at a Boston conference sponsored by Forrester Research, a computing industry consulting firm) that Microsoft missed the developing importance of the Internet. They missed it! Completely missed it.[18]

b. Again, it's not just technology-driven change that's difficult to predict. For example, tomato-infused Heinz missed the early success of salsa (the condiment, not the dance) as a mass-market product. And Microsoft, Google and others missed the early huge growth in social networking. And it was Bruegger's, a relatively new entrant to the bagel business, and not the many local bagel bakeries that catapulted bagels from an ethic food generally only available in larger U.S. cities to a mass-market product.

c. It seems almost impossible that existing firms missed major changes in the fields in which they were dominant – but it speaks to how difficult it is to predict the future.

d. **The greater the uncertainty of change, the more complex the environment**.

C. Drivers.

1. **Number of drivers**. Drivers are the sources of change. Important here is that the number of drivers in the environment is potentially huge.

a. For example, let's think about the athletic shoe industry and a company like Nike. Nike needs to attend to. . .

(1) the fashion tastes of kids and adults throughout the world,

(2) the actions of dozens of other athletic shoe producers (some in the US and some in other countries),

(3) the financial markets,

(4) the changing patterns of retail distribution and sale,

(5) public concern for the plight of the people who manufacture Nike's shoes in various third world countries (e.g., low wages, child labor, etc.),

(6) bilateral, regional, and world trade regulations,

(7) technology that may affect the making, distribution, or selling of the shoes,

(8) and so on.

b. Any or all of these drivers are subject to rapid, large scale, and/or uncertain change. Each could affect how Nike does business or the profitability of this business.

(1) For example, assume that Adidas found a way to use the Internet to allow you to order custom-designed shoes. Adidas is in Nike's environment. Might that change business conditions for Nike? Probably, and probably in a big way.

(2) Example 2. Assume some country passed a law requiring that local employees of firms selling to U.S. firms receive minimum wages comparable to that earned by employees in the U. S. If Nike shoes were manufactured in that country, could that affect cost of making the shoes? Of course.

c. All things equal, **the greater the number of potential sources of change (i.e., the greater the number of drivers), the more complex the environment.**

2. **Dynamics.** Dynamics refers to the nature of change for a given driver. Think of this as "what causes a source of change to change?"

a. Returning to the above example, the dynamics of change in local wage rates may involve things as varied as world opinion and local politics.

b. For Adidas' potential use of the Internet, the dynamics involve such things as business decisions at Adidas and technical developments in Internet capability, the latter of which is affected by decisions and actions far removed from either Nike or Adidas.

c. It should be obvious that the dynamics of one driver are likely to be quite different from the dynamics of another.

d. **The more varied and complicated the dynamics of the drivers, the more complex is the environment.**

D. Putting all this together.

1. **First, all business environments are complex. The only real issue is how complex.**

a. Table 1-1, located at the end of these notes, provides a simple framework for pulling together all of the above ideas.

b. We will consider rate, magnitude, and uncertainty of change, number of drivers, and driver dynamics as independent, at least in the sense that knowledge of one of these tells us virtually nothing about another.

Table 1–1   Change, Drivers, and the Complexity of the Environment

	DRIVERS **Fewer with less varied and complicated dynamics**	**DRIVERS** **Many with more varied and complicated dynamics**
CHANGE: Slower, smaller, and more predictable	LEAST COMPLEX	INTERMEDIATE
CHANGE: Faster, greater, and less predictable	INTERMEDIATE	MOST COMPLEX

The arrow shows the general trend over the past decade or two. As noted in the text, we can identify both drivers that are specific to a particular firm and drivers that are more general, such as deregulation, globalization, the shift to market economies, the breakdown or many traditional monopolies and oligopolies, and technology.

2. Juxtaposing our discussion of open systems and the complexity of the environment **implies that attending to, anticipating, understanding, responding to, and leading development in complex environments is critical to the success of the firm**.

    a. Over the past two decades, <u>environmental complexity has increased</u>. Hence, various policies that were successful in, say, 1990 or 2000, or even last year, may not be very useful today.

    b. That is, there has been a shift from the LEAST COMPLEX to the MOST COMPLEX boxes in Table 1-1.

    c. There are many reasons for this shift.

        (1) Some are specific to industries or even to specific firms.

        (2) Clearly, we witness today the effects of macroeconomic conditions and technological advances.

        (3) In addition, there are at least five broad trends that tend to affect all (or most) industries and firms. . .

            (a) A general shift toward deregulation,

            (b) A general trend toward market-driven economies,

            (c) The breakup of traditional monopolies and oligopolies,

            (d) Globalism, and

            (e) Technology.

        (4) In my opinion, two other longer term trends <u>may</u> be in the early phases:

            (a) A return by households and firms to a greater level of savings than has been true for many decades (or put another way, to reduce the use of debt as a financing mechanism).

            (b) A growing tendency to believe that asset bubbles are annoyingly common (or put another way, an increasing tendency to better assess the risks inherent in various investments).

            (c) Both of these may be important outcomes of the recent economic crisis.

E. Broad trends involved with increased environmental complexity.

    1. Deregulation: Two classic examples.

        a. **The domestic airline industry**.

            (1) In the 1970s, the environment of the domestic airline industry was not particularly complex. Why? Federal regulation mandated that an airline firm could not change prices, schedules, or routes without government approval. This process took months or years and was more or less public.

                (a) The result was limited head-to-head competition in most markets. If you wanted to fly from New York to Miami, there were only two carriers (as I recall) with nearly identical prices.

                (b) Since neither firm had much uncertainty regarding the other's prices (for example), neither would spend much time nor resources trying to predict the rival's price strategy. Today, that would be like McDonald's not needing to worry whether Wendy's would change the price of their burgers.

                (c) Also, since neither firm had much incentive to devote time or resources to predict the price strategy of a rival, neither firm was likely to know or learn much about how to develop price strategy in competitive markets. Indeed, neither firm was likely to understand what a competitive market was.

            (2) It should be no surprise then, that when airline rates, routes, and schedules were deregulated, the existing players really didn't know how to "do" price strategy.

        b. **The domestic banking industry**.

            (1) Most banks in the 1970s had only one type of personal checking account, again because of regulation. Checks looked the same (none of today's fancy styles) and checking accounts all provided the same service (none of today's various options).

            (2) Since there was virtually no threat of any new checking services, most banks spent neither time nor or resources developing their own new products or services. Today that would be like A&F not having to worry about what new shirt style American Eagle will bring to the market next month.

(3) Because banks had no incentive to devote time or resources to product development or marketing, most knew very little about how to develop or market new products.

(4) Again, it shouldn't be a big surprise that when the domestic banking industry was substantially deregulated, very few existing banks had much skill in product development.

   c. What do we learn from this?

     (1) First, **deregulation is one important cause of the increase in environmental complexity**.

       (a) In the U.S., we've seen deregulation in such industries as domestic airlines, interstate trucking, many aspects of banking, telephone service, electric and natural gas distribution, and so on.

       (b) In the U.S., deregulation can occur at the national or state level. For example, both Pennsylvania and California have deregulated electrical power distribution, but many states have not.

       (c) This can also occur at the international level. An example is the North American Free Trade Agreement (NAFTA), an agreement among Mexico, Canada, and the U.S., which deregulates certain aspects of trade among these countries.

     (2) Second, while this is not the place for an extended discussion, deregulation is the outcome of political action that affects firms by changing important aspects of their environments.

       (a) **This is important as it suggests that governments can, and do, control critical parameters affecting business**.

       (b) Exactly because politics largely shapes regulation, many parties (e.g., firms, customers, trade associations, labor unions, and others) **lobby** to regulate or deregulate certain aspects of the environment consistent with their personal views of expected outcomes.[19]

       (c) In common current language, we often hear about "special interests" extracting undue influence on individual lawmakers (at local, state, and federal levels) leaving the impression that lobbying <u>per se</u> is inappropriate, unethical, or even illegal. However, while Congress has the right to place certain constraints on the lobbying process[20] lobbying <u>per se</u> is protected under the First Amendment's guarantee of the right to petition the government.

     (3) Third, while we can observe a several decade trend toward the broad deregulation of industry in the U.S., we have also observed important cross-currents pushing in the other direction. For example, see the brief discussion of the Sarbanes-Oxley Act later in this chapter. Also, the current economic conditions have produced an aggressive re-entry of the federal government into the affairs of business.

2. The shift toward market-driven economies.

   a. Since about 1990, we have seen a sharp move to **market (or market-driven) economies from centrally-planned ones**.

     (1) For example, the countries of the ex-Soviet Union have been, more or less, moving in this direction. So have China and India.

     (2) In a centrally planned economy, the government usually sets prices, determines product mix, and controls distribution. In market-driven economies, these functions are substantially influenced by the actions of firms and consumers.

       (a) Nations characterized by market-driven economies are called **capitalistic**, and are said to practice **capitalism**.

       (b) In practice, capitalism comes in many forms, determined largely by the degree to which regulation allows market forces to operate.

       (c) If we compare, for example, Germany, Japan, and the U.S., we see different levels of regulation in different markets, and hence, different forms of capitalism.[21]

   b. Generally, it is important to distinguish the economic system from the political system. China, Russia, and India, for example, have adopted some aspects of market-driven economies (or more properly <u>are</u> adapting), but their national political systems operate quite differently from that of, say, the U.S. [22, 23]

3. Other broad trends.
   a. **Globalization** of markets has also contributed to increasing environmental uncertainty.
      (1) Globalization involves not just trade between countries, but also and perhaps more importantly, extensive investment by firms from one country into manufacturing and distribution activities in other countries.
      (2) For example, Japanese automobile manufacturers have made significant investments in plants located in the U.S. So have German carmakers (indeed there is a stretch from Georgia to Alabama that has a huge concentration of not just car makers such as BMW and Mercedes, but also German suppliers such as Bosch).[24]
   b. Two other factors have significantly contributed to increased environmental uncertainty: the **breakup of many traditional monopolies and oligopolies,**[25] and the **rapid pace of technological development**.
4. <u>Bottom line</u>: **Most firms today do business in environments that are much more complex than a decade or two ago**.
   a. For our purposes, we have identified five general contributors: the shift toward market economies, globalization, deregulation, the breakup of many traditional monopolies and oligopolies, and rapid changes in technology, and I speculated on the early emergence of two other possible trends.
   b. Are these "large" forces independent? Equally important?
      (1) Probably "no" to both questions.
      (2) But for the purposes of this class, we'll think of all five as more or less equally important and generally independent, at least in the sense that knowledge about one "force" one tells us virtually nothing about another.
   c. I don't think it a stretch to suggest that the environment will continue to become even more complex in the future.
   d. We'll have more to say about all this in various places throughout the rest of these notes.

V. Why is the degree of environmental uncertainty important?

   A. As noted above, firms need to make various decisions and uncertainty makes this more difficult.
      1. For example, firms need to estimate future demand (what to make, how much to make, and how to price), need to determine how to provide supply (this is often called the "make, buy, or lease decision"), need to set prices, and need to distribute products and services.
      2. If environments had no uncertainty, than the outcome of any possible set of actions would be more or less completely predictable.
      3. In that situation, decision-making would be relatively easy-identify all possible courses of action and, given some set of criteria, choose the "best" course (although determining the criteria may also be complicated).
   B. However, all environments have some level of uncertainty.
      1. Hence, the outcome of any set of actions is **not** known with certainty.
      2. **This is normal** even in low complexity environments.
      3. As the level of uncertainty increases, the evaluation of alternative sets of actions becomes increasingly more difficult. Moreover, no one technology exists which can completely integrate all of this complexity.[26]
      4. While this may have been relatively more unusual twenty or even ten years ago, today it is the standard situation.
   C. So, what are the effects of the degree of environmental uncertainty?
      1. **How the firm makes decisions** may change, including what criteria are used. This is true not just for firms but also for the general public. A great example here is watching as firms attempt to determine the degree to which important stakeholders (the concept of stakeholders is developed below) expect the firm to increase the importance placed by the firm on sustainability and environmental protection.
      2. **What choices** the firm actually makes may change. That GM recently decided to axe the Pontiac and Saturn brands was probably not even a choice under serious consideration five years ago.

3. Exactly since the future is difficult to anticipate, existing firms will more often make serious mistakes, **resulting in the increased likelihood of failure of existing firms**.

4. And since all this uncertainty tends to generate new situations, **it provides fertile new opportunities, both for new firms to emerge and for existing firms able to quickly react**.

D. In this course, we will revisit these issues several times. Many subsequent courses will focus in detail on (a) understanding the level of uncertainty in a firm's environment and (b) learning the tools, techniques, and concepts with which to make decisions under different levels of uncertainty. But for now, at least we have a developing concept of what a "complex environment" is.

VI. And what about "managing"?

A. Managing and management.

1. **Management**, as used in this course, is a noun referring to a set of employees with particular types of responsibilities, discussed below, while **managing** refers to the actions used to satisfy these responsibilities. Although the two words are very similar, we have to be careful how we use them.

2. Two important concepts: <u>responsibility and authority</u>.

a. **Responsibility** is a workplace obligation or duty that must be accomplished or discharged.

(1) **All** employees have responsibilities.

(2) Responsibilities vary. This variation helps us distinguish the members of the management team from members of the non-management team.

(3) I think in terms of four different kinds of responsibilities:

(a) Those involving **personal accomplishments** ("I am responsible for opening the shop tomorrow").

(b) Those involving **the accomplishments of other people** ("I am responsible for getting the orchestra to evoke a certain mood").

(c) Those involving **tactical business issues** ("I am responsible for getting our new product to market on time, on spec, and on budget").

(d) Those involving **strategic business issues** ("I am responsible for expanding his firm's business into Brazil").

(4) "Tactical" refers to business issues affecting the current operations of the firm, while "strategic" refers to the longer-term operations.

(5) Although distinctions between these four types of responsibility are often vague, they help us to distinguish among non-management employees, supervisors, managers, and general managers by the relative importance of responsibilities. (Please see Table 1-2.)

(6) Since all employees have some responsibilities, all employees manage something, even if only themselves. However, the term "management" usually means those identified in Table 1-2 as either managers or general managers. Sometimes it includes first line supervisors and sometimes does not.

Table 1-2 Relationships between Relative Responsibilities and Types of Managers★

	Responsibility for . . .			
	Personal Accomplishments	**Accomplishments of Other People**	**Tactical Business Issues**	**Strategic Business Issues**
Non–Management	XXXXX	X	X (?)	?
Supervisor★★	XXXXX	XXX	XX	X
Manager	XXXXX	XXXX	XXX	XX
General Manager	XXXXX	XXXXX	XXXXX	XXXXX

★ Xs represent the relative magnitude of the responsibility and/or the relative importance of the responsibility at this level.

★★Various federal agencies use the term "Supervisor" in specific legal terms. Because of the nature of legalisms, it is possible that a manager is not a supervisor. This is an unusual case and need not bother us here.

    b. The second term is **authority**.

        (1) For our purposes, authority refers to certain "rights" the firm builds into a position. What kind of rights?

            (a) Rights to make certain decisions.

            (b) Rights to commit certain resources of the firm.

        (2) For example, the university grants me the right to make certain decisions regarding the content of my courses. That is, I have the authority to design my classes more or less as I believe they should be designed. This is not true for all U.S. universities.

    c. Often you hear employees say that they do not have sufficient authority to discharge their responsibilities.

        (1) First, this is a common situation.

        (2) You could interpret this as a basic flaw in the design of the firm. From this perspective, the "solution" is to increase authority or decrease responsibility (or both).

        (3) A different view is that this is a useful source of innovation within the firm. The argument is as follows:

            (a) Authority is the right to make certain decisions and to commit certain resources of the firm. The amount of resources that a firm has is finite.

            (b) Everyone in the firm would like more authority, either to satisfy his/her responsibilities or to build a "cushion."

            (c) If the "sum" of authority sought by the firm's personnel exceeds the firm's total resources, then authority is a scarce resource.

            (d) Scarcity often forces individuals to find new ways of satisfying a responsibility, perhaps by using fewer resources or inventing completely new ways to accomplish the responsibility.

            (e) In my opinion, exactly because authority is limited (in the sense of a scarcity of decision making rights and/or resources to commit), **each of us has incentives to be innovative in accomplishing our responsibilities**.

            (f) Sometimes this leads to problems (an "innovative" solution could be illegal or unethical), but often it leads to positive new ways to meet these responsibilities. Indeed, often the really exciting part of a job is figuring out "better ways" to get the job done (i.e., to satisfy your responsibilities) without additional resources.

3. Management activities.

    a. The literature contains many lists of the activities of managers.[27] Typical inclusions on these lists are such activities as coordinating, controlling, planning, and communicating.

    b. The basic idea behind these older lists of activities was the belief that performing these specific activities well would improve the likelihood of the long-term success of the firm given the opportunities and the threats posed by the environment.

    c. When environments were less complex, managing was probably more straightforward, exactly since fewer things in the environment required attention, and those things that did require attention were likely to change less rapidly, and in smaller, more predictable ways.

    d. In that world, the view was that nearly all managers in a firm were responsible for some relatively narrow aspect of the current or near-term operations of the firm. A few had primary responsibility for the long-term operations of the firm. In this scheme, non-managers were responsible only for their own personal outcomes.

    e. This produced a pyramidal organization structure called bureaucracy.[28]

    f. This traditional view is changing, however, as environments have gotten more complex.

        (1) Increasingly firms have expanded the responsibility of non-managers through a process called **empowerment**.[29] A similar process has also tended to increase the responsibilities of managers, so that many more now have to be concerned with both the current and the long-term operations of the firm.[30]

      (2) Some people view empowerment as a fad, while others think it serious.

      (3) This is a topic that most of you will examine in your organizational behavior or human resource management courses.

4. Given that the environment today is, generally, more complex than in the past, I don't find it useful to focus on lists of activities. Rather, I think in terms of problems that must be solved, who has the responsibility for what part of the solution, and who can commit resources.

    a. Following from March and Simon,[31] I assume that the vast majority of problems faced by the firm and its employees (at all levels) are more or less "routine."

    b. Routine means "we've faced this problem—or something very similar to it—many times before." For example, firms routinely have to price new products.

    c. However, as environments get increasingly complex, the number of "new" problems (problems we have not seen before) increases.

5. For most of firm's routine problems, more or less standard solution techniques, called **heuristics**, exist. That is, firms develop heuristics, or routine solution techniques, for solving "routine" problems.

    a. These techniques don't guarantee perfect solutions. But, they do provide a structured and efficient (i.e., low cost) approach to routine problems with some acceptable quality of solution.

    b. Although we will learn about some of these routine problems and outline some of the solution techniques, our **main purpose** in this course is providing a conceptual sense of the problems, and why they are problems, rather than on solutions. This conceptual sense is part of the big picture view discussed in the introduction.

    c. **Later business courses** will develop many of these problems more precisely and present various solution techniques.

      (1) For example, one routine business problem of most firms is the "break even" problem. This asks how many things do we have to make and sell in a period of time to "just break even," given various costs, constraints, and competitive forces.

      (2) We'll develop this problem as one aspect of our conceptual discussion of pricing (Chapter 5), and we'll even have a few numerical examples to work through.

      (3) You may have seen "break even" problems in microeconomics and you'll see it again in managerial accounting.

6. Although routine problems are probably the most common type of problems faced by the firm, "new" problems emerge all of the time.

    a. For example, over the past few years many firms have had to face the problems posed by e-commerce (should we? for what part of our product set? for which customers? how? how fast?).

    b. At first, new problems tend to be treated as "exceptions," exactly because the firm has no experience with them. Sometimes existing heuristics are applied to new problems and sometimes they provide acceptable solutions. But many new problems require fundamentally new solution methods.

    c. When first used, new solutions are often inconsistent, inefficient, and annoying, again exactly because they are not part of the routine of the firm. However, if the new problem persists, the firm gains experience with it and new heuristics emerge.

    d. Usually, new but recurring problems rapidly become routine ones, and new heuristics emerge.

B. Given all this, I propose the following as a general definition of managing:

    1. "Managing" is

       • the more or less standard application

       • of more or less standard tools

       • to more or less standard problems

       • using more or less standard criteria

       • to evaluate the effectiveness of proposed solutions and the efficiency of resource utilization within an individual's domain of responsibility, subject to the constraints of authority,

       • given that new problems may require fundamentally new approaches.

2. Reflection on the above.
   a. Sorry if this definition makes managing sound dull. Sometimes it is, but it usually isn't. Remember, the basics of many exciting human endeavors from eating to enjoying music to skiing are, more or less, standard. That doesn't mean that they are dull and lifeless.
   b. **"More or less standard . . ." doesn't mean simple or obvious**.
      (1) Rather, it implies the existence of a well-developed set of problems, a well-developed set of applicable tools and techniques, and a well-developed set of criteria. As noted above, the break-even problem is one example. Others include. . .
         (a) The "capital budgeting problem," which concerns whether a firm should invest in this or that (or no) long-term project, given expected costs, expected benefits, the time value of money, the cost of capital (i.e., costs associated with the money used), tax effects, and perhaps other issues.
         (b) The "make, buy, lease problem," which concerns whether the firm should make a product for sale using owned facilities, buy it already made for resale, or lease facilities to make it.
      (2) I assume that most effective employees know these and can judge which problems they face, what tools to use, and what criteria to apply. Much of your academic experience will teach these to you. Others will be learned on the job.
      (3) However, if all business opportunities were all perfectly obvious to all parties all of the time, many employees would be unnecessary. Mechanical or electronic analyses would suffice.
      (4) Since each firm has (a) a unique environment and (b) different competencies, goal sets, histories, and expectations of the future, each tends to have a unique interpretation of what "more or less standard" means.
         (a) This implies that standard problems are addressed and treated differently by different firms, and, probably even by the same firm at different times.
         (b) This is a topic about which numerous authors have developed interesting observations— two that I like are by Douglass North and by Larry Greiner.[32]
3. Finally, let's remember, everyone, managers and non-managers alike, manages something, even if only their personal work responsibilities.

VII. So, let's put the pieces together. What does "**managing in complex environments**" mean?

Managing in complex environments means knowing, understanding, and discharging one's work place responsibilities, within the authority granted by the firm, in business environments characterized by many complex drivers that are subject to rapid, large-scale, and hard-to-predict changes.

VIII. Goals of the firm.
   A. Earlier, I said that firms are social structures with deliberately structured tasks, boundaries and goals having a legal existence and identity, responsibilities and obligations, and at least some concern with the creation of wealth.
      1. We have just spent considerable time talking about boundaries, and the difference between managing (which we assume originates "inside" the firm's boundary) and the environment (which we assume to be "outside" the boundary). We also hinted at the nature of a relationship between the two (actually all we said was that as the environment has gotten more complex, so has the challenge of managing the firm).[33]
      2. This seems like a good time to discuss the goals of the firm and the criteria by which to evaluate whether these goals are being met.
   B. How many goals does a firm have?
      1. There are two major schools of thought.
         a. A business firm has one goal: to maximize the wealth of the owners.
         b. A business firm has more than one goal.
      2. Let's walk through these two arguments.

C. Firms have one goal expressed either as "maximize the wealth of the owners of the firm" or "maximize profit."[34]

   1. Assume that as the entrepreneur and sole owner of the firm, I make decisions concerning products, prices, people, and production so as to yield the greatest returns to me. Why not? I put up the capital, had the idea, and bear the risk associated with loosing my capital or not making best use of it. Open and shut case, no? Well, maybe yes, but maybe no. Some possible problems are discussed below.

   2. First, not-for-profit entities are not profit maximizing "by definition."

   3. Second, the relative importance of profit maximizing by firms may vary by nation.[35]

   4. Third, even if firms wish to maximize profits, it may be difficult for the entrepreneur to implement the proper courses of action to produce maximum profits.

     a. First, complex environments are not completely predictable. At best, many critical decisions depend on estimates of the future (e.g., estimating future demand for this or that product at this or that price).

     b. Second, often parties other than the entrepreneur have input to these decisions (or the estimates on which these decisions are based).

       (1) For example, the entrepreneur may require a loan to assist the start-up of the business. When this occurs, the lender usually prefers a more conservative approach to investment decisions in order to increase the likelihood that the loan will actually be paid back.

       (2) However, exactly because the presence of loans means "some other person's money is at risk," the entrepreneur may wish to pursue a more risky path than if only his or her money were involved.[36]

       (3) That is, <u>lender and entrepreneur may be differently sensitive to risk</u>. Not surprisingly, then, they may also differ in preferred courses of action.

       (4) Actual decisions may represent some complex compromise, which may not be profit maximizing from the entrepreneur's perspective.

     c. Third, the actions of others may adversely impact wealth generation.

       (1) The entrepreneur usually hires others to assist in the conduct of the firm's business.

       (2) These employees may wish to maximize their own personal returns. To do so, they may engage in actions that increase their personal returns at a reduction in the entrepreneur's returns. For example, many people choose to "goof off" rather than work when no one is watching. Or do things that enhance their own income or careers rather than what they should be doing.

       (3) This is particularly problematic for employees who may be in a position to effect significant firm policies that improve their own pay, job security, ease of work, etc.

       (4) In economics and finance, this is called the **agency problem**.[37]

     d. Fourth, it may be impossible, in a practical sense, to determine what course of action will produce maximum profits.

       (1) Humans have limited capacity to collect and process information.[38]

         (a) Hence, it may be difficult (or impossible) to collect and assess all information necessary to maximize profits.

         (b) Therefore, firms may seek acceptable solutions rather than optimal solutions. March and Simon coined the term "**satisficing**" to distinguish seeking acceptable solutions from **maximizing**, or seeking optimal solutions.

       (2) Even if we could collect and process all this information, our business exists in a competitive world.

         (a) Hence, our outcomes are determined not just by our actions, but also partly the result of actions taken by competitors whose behavior is not completely predictable.

         (b) A really interesting body of study, called **game theory**, has evolved to address the question of optimal choice of action for firm A given possible actions by competitor B. This is usually a topic covered in advanced economics courses, although you may also see it in business strategy courses.

(3) Also, as noted above, the inherent uncertainty in the environment may make it impossible to identify profit-maximizing actions exactly, forcing the use of probabilistic returns to make decisions.

   e. Fifth, even though economic theory has a richly developed theory of how economic actors should make such decisions, a large body of literature suggests they often deviate from the central assumption of economic rationality.[39]

5. Bottom line: <u>Firms may want to maximize, and in certain cases for certain markets this may be possible. However, the position taken here is that most firms most of the time do not maximize wealth (or profit). This, by itself, does not mean that firms have more than one goal</u> – we now turn to the arguments regarding more than one goal.

D. The alternative: Firms have more than one goal.

1. Many different ways of developing this view. To me, the most interesting is to premise that all firms have unique histories and therefore all firms may (in theory) have unique sets of primary goals.

   a. That firms are all unique is not difficult to argue. They have different founders, different initial conditions, different resources producing relative strengths and weaknesses, different employees, and face different environments.

   b. That these should cause firms to each be somewhat different in terms of goals seems reasonable. (See the North paper cited earlier.)

2. Several possibilities exist that produce different packets of goals.

   a. Different entrepreneurs may have different personal ideas regarding the appropriate set of goals. Some may stress only self-interest, while others may have concerns about the environment, society at large, the local community, their employees' interests and welfare, affecting national policy, and so on.

   b. In large publicly held firms, there is likely to be disagreement among the various stockholders (i.e., the owners), various debt-holders, and others about the specific goals of the firm (as discussed above). Negotiation among these parties (or their representatives) may produce various different goals.

     (1) An interesting side note here is that the general public, either directly or via pension plans, tends to be the "owners" of public corporations in the U.S.

       (a) Most of these holdings are in the form of mutual funds and other vehicles, which have professional managers.

       (b) Action by these managers as they try to produce funds with strong performance (given the various objectives of different funds) may significantly affect the goals of these firms.

     (2) In Japan, historically the general public does not participate heavily in the stock market. Rather the major players are other firms. (Please note: I think this still true, although changing.)

       (a) Usually, firms that have holdings in another firm also have long standing business relations with the "other" firm, either as suppliers, customers, banks, or strategic allies.

       (b) Therefore, in Japan, we may expect the goals of a given firm to reflect these relationships (which have been tested severely by Japan's economic troubles of the past decade).

     (3) In Germany, the major players are often banks with significant debt holdings in the firms in which they own stocks. Individual states within Germany are also sometimes important stockholders of firms whose major facilities are within their borders (this, too, is in transition).

     (4) <u>Bottom line</u>: It shouldn't surprise you that these differences in major stockholders may cause U.S., Japanese, and German firms to have somewhat different goals. For example, U.S. fund managers tend to emphasize some combination of capital appreciation over time and current income (dividends), while affiliated firms in Japan tend to emphasize stable, predictable relationships, and banks in Germany tend to want slow but stable growth.[40]

   c. In both large and small firms, employees (especially senior managers) often have personal goals that are different from those of the owners.

     (1) Negotiation among these parties (or their representatives) may produce various different goals.

     (2) This situation was introduced briefly above as the "agency problem."

      d. Finally, there are many other parties, such as the debt-holders (as discussed above), the community, the customers, the suppliers, governmental bodies, and employees at large. Negotiation among these various "**stakeholders**" and others may also influence goals.

E. **So, what are the goals of business?**

> 1. For the purposes of this course, I will assume that firms usually have multiple goals, which likely vary across firms.

      a. These multiple goals are likely to vary across firms and time.

      b. I assume the goal agenda emerges from a political process involving some, but not all stakeholders. The phrase "**dominant coalition**" refers to the stakeholder subset actually involved in setting this agenda.

      c. The outcome of this process is a set of more or less agreed-to rules. These **governance** rules are used to govern the firm's goals and who shares in the firm's profit stream. We will have much to say this as we move through the course.

> 2. Having said this, I will also assume that in most U.S. firms most of the time, profit emerges as either the dominant goal or at least a dominant goal, even if profit maximizing isn't usually possible.

IX. So what is profit?

  A. A starting point.

    1. **The basic definition of profit is revenues minus expenses**.

    2. Having said that, economists and accountants use the concept of profit in different ways. At issue is what "counts" as revenues and as expenses.

  B. Economic profit.

    1. Most of you have had an economics course. In economics, "profit" or "economic rent" or just **rent** is the ". . . income that is surplus over and above the costs of all the inputs required for production."[41]

    2. No surprises so far. But does this differ from accounting profit (which we call **net income**)?

  C. Comparing accounting profit (net income) and economic profit (rent).

    1. First, accounting standards vary by country. Each country defines revenue and expense differently.[42] Hence, net income will vary by country. This is less likely for rent.

    2. Second, net income is historical, while rent is usually concerned with both the past and the future.

    3. Third, accounting profit is viewed over fixed periods, typically one quarter and one year. Economic profit is usually viewed over a longer indefinite term (backward and forward), which typically exceeds one year.

    4. Fourth, net income usually does not adjust for the **time value of money**, while rent usually does. The time value of money allows us to recognize that the value of $1 today exceeds the value of $1 received one year from now (or, theoretically, one minute from now) due to inflation.

    5. Fifth, publicly held firms (i.e., those whose stock trade publicly) must report net income (among other, more detailed financial data) via a system standardized by federal regulation. There is no current requirement for firms to disclose economic profit, although some provide an estimate.[43]

    6. Sixth, net income does not consider **opportunity costs**, or the effect that committing financial resources to one course of action means those monies will not be available for other, more attractive, uses that may emerge later. Rent often does.

    7. Economic profit considers the **cost of capital**, while accounting profit usually does not. This is a complex concept beyond this course, but the general concept reflects the observation that money raised by the firm to make investments is not free.

    8. Please see Table 1-3 for a summary. **Not surprisingly, accounting and economic profit differ, often dramatically, depending on choices made regarding the above issues.**[44]

with the city's commercial and industrial base, suffice to say that it has reasonably well managed the shift from heavy manufacturing to a more broadly-based economy. It has many unresolved problems, to be sure, but it makes a nice home base and a really great source of examples. Recently, Pittsburgh celebrated its 250th anniversary, making it one of the older U.S. cities, and as such has been a central player in much of the country's history (check out the Senator John Heinz History Center www.pghhistory.org). For a great seven-minute historical tour of the town, try YouTube (www.youtube.com/watch?v=o75yBx8XBK0&feature=player_embedded#).

4. On November 29, 2007, the firm announced its acquisition by Fresenius Medical Care AG & Co. KGaA, a German firm described as "the largest integrated global provider of dialysis products and services." (Please see the Renal Solutions Inc. press release at http://www.renalsolutionsinc.com/home/newsandevents.html.)

5. And, in case you didn't already know, the UPMC Kidney Transplant Program, under the direction of Dr. Ron Shapiro, is one of the leading programs in the world.

6. For an overview of the economic crisis from September 7 to November 15, 2008, see http://www.nytimes.com/interactive/2008/09/27/business/economy/20080927_WEEKS_TIMELINE.html

7. Business failure can result in bankruptcy (which could be in many forms including reorganization or liquidation), in fire-sale acquisition by another firm, or in the most recent period, significant involvement of the federal government. Some high visibility bankruptcies during the current recession include Lehman Brothers, Circuit City, Sharper Image, The Tribune Company (owner of the major newspapers in Chicago and Los Angeles and the Chicago Cubs baseball team), and Polaroid. Merrill Lynch and Wachovia were acquired under duress by Bank of America and by Wells Fargo. JPMorgan acquired a beleaguered Bear Sterns and Washington Mutual (the country's largest Savings and Loan and the country's biggest bank failure ever). Chrysler and General Motors both sought bankruptcy protection, and as part of their restructuring GM will kill off the Saturn and Pontiac brands, and will probably shut down Hummer and Saab if they can't find buyers.

8. Perhaps the phrase you've used is "profit maximization." Wealth and profit are related but not the same thing: wealth is the accumulation of profit over time, or another way of putting it is profit is the period change in wealth. Sounds like a calculus relationship, eh? (Uh-oh.)

9. Having said that, most larger not-for-profit firms are managed much like for-profit ones. And when I say "larger," many not-for-profits can grow to be very large. For example, UPMC (the University of Pittsburgh Medical Center) is one of the region's largest employers.

10. The standard forms of legal existence in the US are corporations, partnerships, and sole proprietorships, although we have seen the evolution of many new forms (e.g., the LLC) in recent years. Unlike most countries, the legal basis for U.S. firms is at the state, not the federal level.

11. For example, the right to hire employees and the obligation to pay taxes.

12. As we will see later in these notes, owners of a firm are one example of a party who has (or believes they should have) some claim on the profit stream of the firm. This broader class is called "stakeholders," and hence owners are one example of a stakeholder group. Others include customers, suppliers, neighbors, and so one. While we're at it, owners may also be called by other terms, dependent in part on the form of legal existence of the firm (for example, owners of a corporation are shareholders of the corporation).

13. The January 4, 2007 *Wall Street Journal* said of Mr. Nardelli's termination:

    "What Mr. Nardelli missed, however, is that in the post-Enron world, CEOs have been forced to respond to a widening array of shareholder advocates. . . .it's in that role that Mr. Nardelli failed most spectacularly."

    Later in the article, they offer a comparison they compare Mr. Nardelli to Mr. Lafley, CEO of Proctor & Gamble about whom the author says "(i)nstead of catering just to shareholders, he makes a broad appeal to 'stakeholders' . . ."
    Both quotes from: https://sslvpn.pitt.edu/pqdweb,DanaInfo=proquest.umi.com+?index=5&did=1189150201&SrchMode=1&sid=1&Fmt=3&VInst=PROD&VType=PQD&RQT=309&VName=PQD&TS=1168019831&clientId=17454 (Accessed January 4, 2007).

14. Some (including me) would argue that, indeed, Dell has lost its edge over the past few years, at least in part because its products seem dull to many buyers. Recent changes in senior management suggest serious continuing problems (see Richtel, M. "2 Executives Leaving in Dell Restructuring," *New York Times*, January 1, 2009, p. B9).

15. By comparison, in Fall 2006 J&R Music World advertised the Toshiba Satellite M-65-S9092 Notebook with Intel® Pentium® M Centrino 2 GHz Processor featuring a 17" active matrix TFT LCD widescreen, 1 gig of DDR2 SDRAM memory, a 100-gig hard drive, a DVD+-RW/CD-RW combo drive, with wireless, Ethernet, and modem connectivity, a multi-format memory card reader and more. Put simply, maybe—twenty to thirty times the machine at about $2000 less (www.JandR.com). And that was four years ago!

16. For an interesting discussion of different rates of change in different industries please see Robert Grant, *Contemporary strategy analysis* (4th ed.), 2002, Oxford, England: Blackwell, pp. 327–329.

17. How old were you in August 1995? eBay didn't yet exist!

18. At the same meeting were the guys who started Netscape, at that point the dominant browser. I could be wrong, but as I remember it, Gates shot them a glance that "sounded" to me like, "Yeah, we missed and you didn't . . . but just wait. . . ." And as you know, Microsoft's Explorer completely eclipsed Netscape a few years later.

19. The sheer size of the lobbying effort is massive – CQ Political MoneyLine reports $2.1 billion spent on federal level lobbying in 2004 (I don't have a specific cite, but the data were reported in http://thinkprogress.org/2006/01/09/lobbying-in-america/ (accessed on December 28, 2007).

20. In 1954, the Supreme Court in United States v. Harriss (347 U.S. 612) found that the basic provisions of the Federal Regulation of Lobbying Act were not "too vague and indefinite" and did not violate the First Amendment of the Constitution.

21. Regulatory differences between nations (and in some instances between states within nations) can be extensive. Essentially, this implies that the environment for firms varies by nations (Or states within nations). This, in turn, implies that there is no such thing as a level playing ground across nations. For example, within the EU, the corporate tax rate in Ireland is significantly lower than in Germany. Did this make Ireland a more attractive place to do business? If we consider only tax rates, then the answer is probably "yes." However, we need to consider the entire set of possible regulatory differences – if we do that we may reach a different answer. In the US particularly this extends also to the states, as each state has a separate legal system and we often observe remarkably different regulatory differences. Another way of saying this is that the environment for business differs significantly within the US depending on state.

22. An important debate concerns the relationship between the "rule of law" and economic growth. While not new (F.A. Hayek wrote one of the important modern treatises – *The Constitution of Liberty* in 1960 <University of Chicago Press; ISBN 978-0-226-32084-7> and many would point to John Locke, writing in the latter half of the seventeenth century), events of the past ten to twenty years have reinvigorated and animated the discussion. This is not the place to review this, but for a good introduction, please see *The Economist*, "Order in the Jungle," March 13, 2008.

23. A Goldman Sachs report in 2003 introduced the acronym BRIC to refer to these three countries plus Brazil and speculated that these BRIC countries would be more significant economic players by 2050 than many of today's major economies. If this interests you, please see the Goldman Sachs' article (Global Economics Paper No: 99, "Dreaming with BRICs: The path to 2050") available at http://www2.goldmansachs.com/ideas/brics/book/99-dreaming.pdf.

24. For an interesting discussion of just how complex the global automobile industry has gotten, please see T. Zaun, G. White, N. Shirouza, and S. Miller, "Two way street: Auto makers get even more mileage from third world," *the Wall Street Journal*, July 31, 2002, pp. A1, A8. Toward the end of the article, there is a discussion of the Zafira, a car made by Opel. Opel is a German manufacturer owned by General Motors; the Zafira is assembled in Thailand for sale in Europe using parts in made in many different countries. Apparently customers don't mind: "Lesley Baert . . . from outside Brussels (Belgium) said he didn't know until Opel told him . . . (that his Zafira) was made in Thailand. 'I thought it was made in Poland'" (p. A8). Just to add to the complexity, GM/Opel now makes a version of the Zafira for Subaru for sale in Japan. One model, two versions, and three continents. (Please note: I added this footnote in 2002, and I don't know if any of these relationships still exist.)

25. We examine monopoly and oligopoly in Chapter 2.

26. See, for example, H. Courtney, J. Kirkland, and P. Viguerie, "Strategy under uncertainty," *Harvard Business Review*, November-December, 1997. Courtney, et al., discuss four levels of uncertainty that a firm may face and discuss the technologies available to decision-makers facing each level. This is an excellent article and you are encouraged to read it.

27. Henri Fayol proposed an early and still frequently cited list (*General and industrial management*, London: Pitman, 1949, originally published in 1916).

28. A bureaucracy has more characteristics than just shape, including a single chain of command from each position to the top and impersonal, competency-based promotion. In relatively unchanging environments, they can be remarkably effective. Even today, most major firms are, to some degree, bureaucracies.

29. See, for example, R. Wellins, W. Byham, and J. Wilson, *Empowered Teams*, San Francisco: Jossey-Bass, 1991.

30. Increasing responsibility sounds good. But there are many subtle issues here. For example, if a person's responsibilities are increased, should pay also increase? Many people think "yes." But empowerment is based on a concept that implies that enhanced responsibilities are inherently motivating and don't require additional regular pay. Indeed, there is controversy in the organizational behavior literature whether extrinsic motivation (e.g., pay) undermines intrinsic motivation (e.g., job challenge). We can therefore ask: Is empowerment exploitation of the employee or advantageous? A detailed discussion is beyond the scope of this course, but most of you will revisit this question in subsequent courses and in employment situations.

31. James March and Herbert Simon, *Organizations*, 1958, NY: Wiley.

Active Practice for Chapter 1: Managing in Complex Environments

1. In this course, we assume that firms . . .
   a. have a legal existence defined by national law
   b. typically have multiple goals
   c. both of the above
   d. none of the above

2. Environments charaterized by large change . . .
   a. are typically also rapidly changing environments
   b. usually have markets that are unregulated
   c. both of the above
   d. none of the above

3. Please develop the argument that leads to the conclusion that the environment of each firm is unique:

4. Given events of the past few years, the historical success of a firm is likely a good predictor of future success.
   a. true   b. false

5. The open systems hypotheses refers to . . .
   a. the observation that firms are for-profit
   b. the observation that firms must interact with their envirnments
   c. the observation that firms have internal boundaries
   d. all of the above

6. Profit . . .
   a. is the difference between revenue and expenses in a given accounting period
   b. is >0 for an oligopolistic firm
   c. is the accumulation of wealth over time
   d. all of the above

7. In a centrally planned economy, governments usually set prices, determine product mix, and control the means of distribution. In market-driven economies . . .
   a. these functions are substantially influenced by the actions of firms and consumers
   b. governments cannot influence business
   c. both of the above
   d. none of the above

8. Assume environmental uncertainty increases from time 1 to 2. Please identify 4 or 5 effects you expect:

9. You're at a talk by a senior executive who says, "We've developed a series of hueristics to respond to the bulk of customer inquiries." You understand this to mean what?

10. In the text, I observe that a lender may be differently sensitive to risk than an entrepreneur. Why?

11. Given the definition/description of game theory in the text, is it likely to be of more importance to monopolies or oligopolies? Why?

12. Identify a number of differences between accounting profit and economic profit.

13. Are stakeholders important to a not-for-profit firm such as the University of Pittsburgh? If yes, please idenitfy as many different stakeholder groups as you can.

14. Please use the following terms in a meaningful sentence: stakeholders, dominant coalition, profit, and governance.

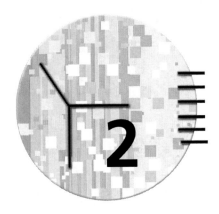

Markets as the Interface Between the Firm and Its Environment

> *Said Simple Simon to the pie man, "Let me taste your ware."*
>
> **Traditional Nursery Rhyme**

I. Teaser.

    A. Even if you never had an economics course, you know a lot about "the market." You buy concert tickets and clothing. You've "sold your labor" to an employer (i.e., held a job). You know how much college textbooks cost. Maybe you've shopped the web for some exotic car. You know that getting free music is a good deal. You know what movies cost and how much your favorite ball player or movie star makes.

    B. Many of you also know that the U.S. stock market went into a serious funk in late 2008, with major indices down 30 to 40 percent and many individual stocks down much more before the recent recovery.

    C. Question: Do the same "rules" affect the price of, say, shoes and stocks?

        1. General answer: yes . . . and no.

        2. Yes, the same general principles affect the prices of all goods and services, and no, there are specific issues that likely affect the price of any particular product or class of products.

    D. Chapter 2 examines the effects of transactions, markets, competitors, and regulatory mechanisms on prices. If you've had microeconomics, much of the territory will be familiar. For those with little or no such background, this may be new stuff. Either way, hopefully you'll have the basic concepts necessary to address the above questions "down pat" by the end of this section.

II. Link to last chapter.

    A. Organizations and environments.

        1. In the last set of notes, we distinguished organizations from their environments, and then we noted that our interest was on a subset of organizations called firms.

            a. Firm are a special type of organization, namely social inventions with boundaries, goals, deliberately structured sets of tasks, a legal existence and identity, rights and responsibilities, and some level of concern with the creation of wealth. Firms may be for-profit or not-for-profit. Our particular interest is with the former.

            b. The complement of the firm in the universe is the firm's unique environment.

        2. We further observed that that all environments are complex to some degree, that complexity has probably increased over the past decade or two, and that it is likely to continue to do so.

        3. Finally, we premised that firms have more or less continuous interaction with their environment ("the "open systems hypothesis.").

B. Each individual in the firm has some role in managing in these complex environments.
  1. These roles vary across individuals.
  2. Variation occurs in terms of . . .
    a. the specific deliberately structured tasks assigned to each person,
    b. the responsibilities built into each position, and
    c. the authority built into each position.
  3. The view taken in these notes is that four generic types of positions can be identified based on responsibilities: regular employees, supervisors, managers, and general managers.
C. We also observed that firms typically have multiple goals.
  1. These goals emerge for many reasons, including the political interplay of the dominant coalition, a subset of the firm's stakeholders, each of whom we assume to have a preferred goal set they wish to superimpose on the firm.
  2. Although firms have multiple goals, all have some interest in the creation of wealth, and hence economic goals are usually particularly important.
  3. Firms tend to develop heuristics to handle routine tasks, and application of these routines combined with information limitations of humans tends to result in firms satisficing rather than maximizing.
  4. The existence of multiple goals results in complex performance criteria for firms.
D. Wealth is the accumulation of profit.
  1. We can distinguish at least two types of profit (economic and accounting).
  2. We assume each group of stakeholders has potentially different preferences about how, and to whom, these profits are distributed.
  3. Political processes, influenced by the dominant coalition, determine how these profits are ultimately distributed over the various stakeholders leading stakeholders to push hard to advance their goals.
  4. Which stakeholder groups participate in the dominant coalition differs from firm to firm and over time within any particular firm.
E. Finally, "governance" is the term to refer to the rules that emerge from the political process for control of the firm's goals and the distribution of the firm's profits. Now we need to expand our understanding of many of these items.

III. Parties and transactions

  A. One company's story
    1. PPG (www.ppg.com) is a Pittsburgh-based firm that makes paints and various other industrial products. Based on material from Chapter 1 and reviewed above, PPG is a for-profit firm with a unique environment, more or less continual interaction with its environment, and so on.
    2. What kinds of interactions does PPG have with its environment?
      a. It sells products to various customers.
      b. It buys various raw and intermediate goods, and it hires employees.
      c. It borrows money from various sources and may lend money to other firms (in the form of commercial paper).
      d. It purchases or leases land, equipment, and buildings.
      e. It pays taxes to governments and dividends to shareholders.
      f. It may buy, sell, or license technology.
      g. It must get rid of its garbage and effluents.
      h. It must adjust policies to be consistent with various laws.
    3. We could go on, but you get the idea. PPG has . . .
      a. A vast number of interactions with its environment.
      b. These occur more or less continuously.
      c. They involve a very large number of different parties in the environment.
      d. Each of these parties is likely to change over time in what it provides to, or wants from, PPG.
    4. In terms of ideas developed last class, PPG operates in a very complex environment.

2. Certainly such agencies are part of the set of things I call regulatory mechanisms. Similarly, we can identify not only state and national level agencies, but also international ones such as the World Trade Organization, established by the General Agreement on Tariffs and Trade.

3. But other mechanisms exist also, at least in my view.
    a. At the other extreme of international agencies is simple human trust, which emerges from ongoing experience or common cultural or religious beliefs.[8]
    b. Trust is potentially very powerful and usually has no out-of-pocket costs, but is relatively easy to exploit.[9] On the other hand, national and international agencies are very expensive to establish and operate, although they may reduce the opportunities for one party to exploit another, or provide a formal means of redress for alleged wrongdoing.

4. These observations allow us to construct a **continuum of regulatory mechanisms** as described in Table 2–1 (at end of these notes).

5. For the purposes of this course, I **assume that the orderliness of markets is due to a combination of the price system and a set of non-price regulatory mechanisms**, potentially unique to each market.

6. For example, consider labor markets. Most employees in the U.S. have an employment relationship based . . .
    a. in part on the price system (my boss and I reach some agreement on what work I will do in exchange for some level of compensation) and
    b. in part on regulatory mechanisms (partly on trust, on contracts, and on state and federal laws).

7. As a practical observation, then, <u>markets usually rely on some combination of the price system and regulatory mechanisms to maintain orderliness</u>.
    a. Please note: This is equivalent to saying that most markets usually don't operate under strict capitalism.
    b. Indeed, as noted in the previous set of notes, nations vary in terms of the extent and form of regulatory mechanisms commonly used, effectively producing multiple "versions" of capitalism.

8. Also note, the existence of regulatory mechanisms introduces costs, which someone must pay. In a few pages, we'll discuss this.

Table 2–1   A Continuum of Regulatory Mechanisms

Regulatory Mechanism	Example	Formality	Cost	Opportunity to Exploit	Redress
International agreements	GATT and World Trade Organization				
National-level statutes and regulations	FDA Act Sherman Anti-Trust Law				
Private law	Contracts	Increasing Formality ↑	Increasing Cost ↑	Increasing Opportunity to Exploit ↓	Greater opportunities for Formal Redress ↑
Industry agreements and standards	League scheduling in professional athletics				
Professional ethics and codes of conduct	Hippocratic oath				
Shared moral and religious codes	"Golden rule"				
Interpersonal trust	History of continued honest dealing				

V. More about the orderliness of markets.

   A. Above I asserted that most markets in developed economies are orderly most of the time. We need to develop this a bit more.

      1. First, "orderly" means that prices, product attributes, and product availability usually don't wildly fluctuate. Please note that this isn't the same thing as saying there is no change.

      2. In the U.S. this is so common, that even slight fluctuations annoy us.

   B. So, why does this orderliness occur?

      1. Well, let's start by going back to our brief discussion above of price theory. If all of those assumptions are met, and the firm is in perfect competition, then:

         a. there is only one generic product, so product attributes are stable,

         b. supply equals demand, so enough product is available, and

         c. price tends to converge to a single equilibrium price, so price is relatively stable.

      2. All of this hinges on . . .

         a. identical public information (recall that all parties, buyers and sellers, know all sellers and the price charged by all sellers), and

         b. unique private information to each party concerning their own preferences and costs/budgets.

         c. If this is true, we say all relevant information is **symmetric**.

      3. But price theory also assumes that each party is self-interested. Self-interested buyers don't want to pay the same as everyone else – they want to pay less. And self-interested sellers don't want the same profit as everyone else (which in a perfect competition is zero) – they want more.

      4. Hence, each party has incentives to acquire information that will give them an advantage in the market – that is, they have incentives to build **asymmetric** information.

      5. If one party does acquire such information, they should be able to "get a better deal" which may lead to market instability and windfall gains to that party.

      6. Whether it is possible to acquire such information is a controversial topic, but given the personal benefits of such information, I tend to believe that it is possible and probably happens often.[10]

   C. However, even given this, markets in developed economies are relatively stable most of the time.

      1. This leads me to believe that "something else" must contribute to market stability other than just price theory.

      2. Which leads me back to regulatory mechanisms and my argument above that the orderliness of markets is due to the joint effect of the price system and regulatory mechanisms.

VI. Competitors.

   A. In any given market, we usually observe more than one seller, more than one buyer, and more than one third party. This isn't always true, as we'll see in a few minutes, but it's a good place to start.

      1. Any party who is on the same side of the transaction as you are in each market in which you participate is your competitor in that market.

         a. If you are a seller, other sellers in that market are your competitors.

         b. If you are a buyer, other buyers in that market are your competitors.

         c. If you are a broker in a particular market, other brokers of the same services in that market are your competitors.

      2. As an example, let's return to the labor market.

         a. The sellers of labor are you guys looking for jobs. Who are your competitors? If there are two of you who want the same job, the answer is obviously "the other guy."

         b. The buyers of labor are employers—if there are two of them and they both want you, are they competitors.

         c. And there are various on-line "job brokers" who are competitors.

      3. I will use the term "rival" to mean a competitor on your sell side.

B. This definition of competitors implies that a party who is your rival in one market may be your ally in another. This is an important idea.

    1. For example, let's consider Ford and Mazda.

        a. Ford and Mazda are competitors (or rivals) in the finished good market (i.e., the market for cars).

        b. However, examination of the old Ford Taurus and the old Mazda MX-6 suggests they had very similar bodies. In fact, they had a common design! In the intellectual property market, Ford and Mazda are partners and the basic design for both cars was a joint project. The whole story is even more complex as Ford owns a chunk of Mazda.[11]

---

    2. KEY POINT: Competition in complex environments frequently involves vigorous competition with rivals in some markets, but close cooperation among the same parties in other markets.

VII. A few general comments about price.

  A. Price is a critical concept in economics, and as we'll see below, economics talks to how prices are set in certain idealized markets (e.g., perfect competition or monopoly).

    1. You probably have some knowledge of these idealized markets, depending on how much economics you have had.

    2. For example, you may know that prices paid by buyers tend to be higher in monopolies than in perfect competition.

    3. Details of how firms actually set prices in markets other than these idealized ones is a topic for later in the course (see Chapter 5).

    4. However, for now we need to observe that prices tend to reflect <u>supply</u> (the amount of a good or service that sellers provide given they could get certain prices), <u>demand</u> (the amount of a particular good or service at a particular price that buyers wish to purchase), <u>attributes</u> of the product or service (size, color, quality, neat designs, etc.), and <u>time</u>. You may have heard this in a slightly different form in a microeconomics course: **Price reflects all known information about the good or service**.

  B. Note that this poses a curious set of paradoxes:

    1. The price a firm charges me is influenced not only by me but also by actions of other sellers and other buyers.

    2. The higher the current price, the more a seller may want to produce. But when production (i.e., supply) increases, prices often fall.

    3. The lower the price, the more buyers may choose to purchase. But when purchases (i.e., demand) increase, prices often go up.

VIII. Idealized markets.[12]

  A. Economic theory has extensively examined the workings of several idealized markets.

    1. By "idealized," I mean that they represent certain special, interesting conditions in theory. In practice many real world markets are close enough to one of these idealized markets that many aspects of "real" markets can be understood in terms of the idealized ones. We will consider four:

        a. perfect competition,

        b. oligopoly,

        c. monopolistic competition, and

        d. monopoly.

    2. Descriptively, the various idealized markets differ in two primary ways.

        a. Assumptions about the number of products, and the relative number and size of buyers and sellers. Size is measured by **market share** for producers (the portion of the total market sold by one producer) or **purchase share** (the portion of the total market purchased by one buyer).

        b. Assumptions about information available to buyers and sellers. I discussed this above in the section on "making markets orderly."

Table 2–2   Idealized Economic Markets

Sellers		Buyers					
How Many?	Size	How Many?	Size	How Many Products?	Entry/Exit Barrier	Idealized Market Called . . .	Example (Left Blank for You to Fill in)
Many	Small	Many	Small	1 or several equivalent	None	Pure Competition	
Few	Larger	Many	Small	1 or several equivalent★	May be some	Oligopoly	
One	100%	Many	Small	1 or several equivalent	Major	Monopoly	
One per segment	100% in their segment	Many per segment	Small	1 per segment; At least 2 segments in total market	None in market; major in segment	Monopolistic Competition	

Additionally, all four idealized markets make certain assumptions about information:

- All sellers know the prices being charged by all other producers, know their own technologies (and hence their own costs), and seek maximum profits (given current prices).
- All buyers know the prices charged by all producers, know their own preferences, and seek to gain a maximum set of preferences (given current prices and income).

★ Microeconomics has studied several types of oligopolies. The simplest of these assumes a homogenous product. Others assume branded products perceived differently by different buyers, rapid changes in product, or infrequent, but significant changes in product. For now, we assume the simplest model.

   c. For a summary of these idealized markets, please see Table 2–2 above. Some details follow.
B. Pricing in **perfect competition**.
   1. Many of you have seen this in your microeconomics course. If you felt comfortable with the discussion there, please dig up your old notes or textbook and review it. Otherwise read the following material and, if you have questions, ask.
   2. Recall that earlier in these notes, we discussed price in terms of supply, demand, time, and attributes. Yet in previous economics courses, you probably discussed only supply and demand. So what happened to attribute and time?
      a. Regarding time: The discussion in most introductory economics courses assumes a spot market. Although it follows the same basic principles, determination of price in futures markets is a more complex issue. If you want more on this topic, I suggest you wait for your first finance course and ask your instructor there to provide some guidance.
      b. Regarding attribute: In perfect competition, we assume either **one product** (hence all products offered by all producers have identical attributes) or multiple products, each slightly different, but from the perspective of the buyer these differences are insignificant.
         (1) In the latter case, we say these products are "completely substitutable" or that buyers are "indifferent" to these slightly altered attributes.
         (2) When there is only one product, we call it a commodity product, a homogeneous product, a generic product, or an undifferentiated product.
         (3) For our purposes, all of these terms ("homogenous," "generic," "commodity," "completely substitutable," "undifferentiated," and "products about which consumers are indifferent") will be used interchangeably.
   3. Price in perfect competition results from the mutual action of sellers (by how much they chose to provide at different potential selling prices) and buyers (by how much they would choose to buy at different prices).

a. Another way of saying this is that, in perfect competition, sellers have little or no control over prices. Offhand, this may seem strange. Why would a seller choose to participate in a market in which they have little or no control over the prices they can charge? As we'll soon see, sellers often try to "escape" situations of perfect competition for exactly this reason (and other reasons also).

b. **We need to be cautious here.** When I say that sellers have little or no control over prices, what I mean is the following:

    (1) A seller can set any price he or she wants.

    (2) However, buyers (since we assume that they know the prices of all producers as noted above) will shop those sellers with the lowest prices (remember, since the products are homogeneous the only interest to the buyer is price).

    (3) This tends to push the prices charged by all sellers downward and toward a common figure so that can actually sell their products.

c. However, sellers incur production costs, and they are not usually interested in selling below what it cost them to make the product.

    (1) Indeed, sellers want to make a profit.

    (2) This also tends to move prices higher.

d. Is it possible to have a situation in which the number of producers is so large and the amount of supply so great that knowledgeable buyers can "force" producers to drop prices below the cost of manufacture?

    (1) Yes.

    (2) What happens then? Some producers are forced out. This is another reason why sellers try to avoid or escape perfect competition.

    (3) But what happens when producers get forced out?

        (a) There are fewer sellers, and hence less product on the market.

        (b) If buyer demand stays constant, prices tend to move upward as buyers compete with each other for the opportunity to buy the product.

e. Let's try an example. (I'm using a 2004 Steeler example.)

    (1) In 2004, the Steelers made a run at the Super Bowl XXXIX.

        (a) Before the Jets game, many people wanted Steeler hats, T-shirts, and so on. T-shirts are a business that has many small producers. Hence, they began to produce as many as possible (so we have a large number of smaller producers, one of the conditions for perfect competition).

        (b) There are many Steeler fans in Pittsburgh, but most of them will only buy a few shirts (hence, we have a large number of customers, none of them very large, a second condition for perfect competition).

        (c) Although T-shirts are all a bit different, most of the differences are of limited interest to fans. Basically, most fans just want a T-shirt that says "Steelers" (even if not an officially licensed design). Hence, assume customers are indifferent to these variations—the product is more or less a commodity, a third condition for perfect competition.

    (2) So, what happened to the prices of these shirts?

        (a) Demand for these shirts was very high during the first week of the playoffs.

        (b) Indeed, demand in the first week may have exceeded the total number that all producers could make.

        (c) So, what happened to price?

- It was high.
- Why? As buyers competed with each other for the limited supply (remember, earlier we saw that buyers compete with each other), sellers could charge high prices and many buyers would still buy the shirts.
- How high could the prices go? It depends completely on how much the buyers were willing to pay.
- However, we assume that as prices move upward, fewer and fewer fans would be willing to pay the higher and higher prices.

- Hence, prices would tend to stabilize at some relatively high level. As it turns out, this level is exactly the price at which fans would buy all available shirts. Some fans would not have shirts because they were unwilling to buy at the high price, but sellers would be happy, because they could sell out at high prices.

(3) Assuming that the Steelers might "go all the way," and that as Super Bowl fever increased, more fans would buy shirts (or a second one), producers tended to increase their production just waiting for more good times.

(4) Then, boom. The Steelers lost to New England (again). Now what happened?

   (a) Fan demand for shirts plummeted. Lots of shirts out there, but very few buyers.

   (b) What happened to prices now?

   - They fell.
   - How low?
   - Generally as low as needed to induce fans to buy them.
   - Might the price drop below the cost of producing them? Certainly. This is not what the sellers want, but it could happen? Sure.
   - What is the result? Now fans could pick up real bargains making them happy. Sellers, however, are glum, because they may actually be losing money.

(5) Bottom-line observations:

   (a) In perfect competition, prices move up and down as the relative supply and demand of a commodity product changes.

   (b) Hence, price is determined by the joint action of buyers and sellers, and individual sellers have limited or no control over prices, except by their choice of how many to make or what attributes to provide.

   (c) Since it takes time to make and to distribute shirts, sellers must estimate demand and decide what attributes to provide **before** actual demand is known. Sometimes they guess correctly, sometimes they don't.[13]

   (d) Moreover, sellers face a dilemma even if they are certain that the Steelers will be in the Super Bowl.

   - The more likely they will be in the finals (and hence the greater the predicted demand), the more shirts each producer may want to make.
   - The result may be that even with extraordinary demand, there may be more shirts on the market than there is demand with the curious result that even with very high demand, prices may stay low.

   (e) If this weren't complicated enough, there is another problem. If projected demand is high, it may induce new producers to enter the market (perhaps to make a quick buck), increasing supply even more and depressing prices yet further. And in perfect competition, we assume entry (and exit) is costless.

4. So what do we learn from all this?

   a. In perfect competition, prices emerge by the joint actions of buyers and sellers. Hence, sellers have little or no real control over prices. All they can do is estimate next period's demand and use this demand estimate to determine how much to supply.

   b. Those of you who have taken microeconomics should recall that in theory, perfect competition results in exactly no long-term profit (or loss) for producers.

   c. In real situations that closely approximate perfect competition, the situation is a little different. In any given period, a given producer may earn profits or incur losses, based on the accuracy of these estimates. However, the average profit over all producers tends toward zero (we can say that the "expected value" of profit in the short run is zero).

   d. However, exactly because the theoretical long-term profit is zero and the expected value in the short run is zero, firms really dislike perfect competition on the product (or output or selling) side.

7. In a more precise sense, then, we can say that <u>product differentiation is an attempt by the firm to shift the risk associated with perfect competition to a new risk associated with developing new products</u>.

   a. Some firms will find this shifting of risk attractive because of a belief that the benefits (relative to costs) of the shift will exceed those of not shifting (and hence slugging it out in perfect competition).

   b. Other firms will not find this shift in risk attractive. Big surprise: Such firms are not likely to be first movers.

8. Is it good or bad for buyers when firms pursue monopolistic competition?

   a. The simple answer is that it has aspects of both, but usually it is more positive than negative for buyers.

   b. Positives.

      (1) The biggest positive is that product differentiation is an "engine of invention" for new products and new product attributes. That is, perfect competition does not produce new products (which many of you may think)—**rather, escape from (or avoidance of) perfect competition may create new products**.

      (2) Another positive is that if the new idea is very popular, other sellers (second movers) will (eventually) enter and may contribute to decreasing prices (which buyers obviously prefer).

   c. At least two negatives.

      (1) The price for the new style T-shirt will likely be higher, at least initially (but presumably at least some buyers won't mind the higher price for something that better suits their interests than the commodity good – which, by the way, is the answer to the question "WHY??" a few pages back).

      (2) However, as competition becomes re-established, there is an incentive to some firms to abandon the "new" attributes and move on to a yet newer product.

         (a) Yesterday's "new" products may become old-hat tomorrow. Yet many buyers purchased the older product and often aren't willing to toss it out just because there is something new "out there." This may become a problem for the buyer if what he/she bought is "abandoned" (or "orphaned") by sellers.

         (b) There are many interesting examples here ranging from software products and video game systems to "fashionable" clothes. One of the classic examples occurred in the early days of VCRs.
            • Sony was first to the market with a VCR using a technology called "Beta Max."
            • For any of a number of reasons, an alternate technology quickly emerged and dominated the market.
            • The result was that people who bought Beta Max devices quickly found no new tapes available. Basically, most people who bought a Beta Max were stuck with a VCR that couldn't play most available tapes.

         (c) Lots of current examples here regarding computer based game boxes and software.

9. While we've raised the idea, let's also introduce (or recall) some terms that will be developed more fully later in the course.

   a. **Product differentiation** is adding (or changing) a product attribute that distinguishes it in some important way from other similar products available in the market.

   b. **Product development** is the process of making investments in **market research** (discussed above) and other product **research and development** (or R&D) with the hope of discovering these new product attributes.

   c. New attributes usually only appeal to some portion of the entire customer base; these "portions" are called **market segments**.

   d. The first firm to differentiate is a **first mover**. The same phrase is also applied to firms that develop reputations as often being the first ones to market with either new products or new product attributes. For example, at one time Sony was "the" first mover in consumer electronics. Apple may now occupy that role.

C. Process enhancement, oligopoly, and monopoly.
   1. The second strategy takes a very different approach.
      a. To develop it, let's return to the same T-shirt situation as before.
         (1) Recall, one of the producers said: "Our shirts are nearly identical to those of other shirt makers. Buyers aren't dumb. They know all of these shirts are more or less substitutable, and knowing this, they're going to buy the least expensive ones."
         (2) (OK, now here's the difference.) "What if we could figure out how to reduce the cost of making T-shirts? If we can reduce the cost by $2, we could lower price and still make a profit. Wow!"
   2. Again we need to make an investment, but this time **the focus will be on enhancement (or "improvement") of the means of production, not on modification of product attributes**.
      a. Product differentiation is an easier concept for most students than is the concept of process enhancement. This is normal since most of you have had much experience with new products, but not nearly as much experience with the manufacturing process.
      b. Hence, a few examples may be useful.
         (1) A firm may invest in new machinery that significantly increases the speed of production.
         (2) A firm may invest in training that improves workforce skill.
         (3) A firm may invest in improved quality control methods that reduce scrap or wasted time.
      c. **Important:** Since the firm began in perfect competition and has not invested in product differentiation, it is still making the "original" generic product.
   3. As was true for product differentiation . . .
      a. the firm has a decision about shifting risk, only this time the focus is reducing cost (or increasing quantity or enhancing capability) by improving the production product process;
      b. these investments are risky because no good solution may be found;
      c. and as before, some firms will find this attractive and others will not.
   4. Let's assume the firm is successful and can reduce costs (remember for the same generic product). What may happen?
      a. We could pass some of this to customers in the form of lower price.
      b. Customers flock to the lower price version of the product (notice the product is not "cheaper" in the sense of less quality).
      c. Other producers must reduce their prices to attract customers.
      d. But since they are in perfect competition and haven't yet made the investments needed to reduce costs, the new price produces negative profits.
         (1) Eventually, this process may cause the less innovative firms to fail, reducing the number of producers.
         (2) As this happens, the market may begin to look more like an **oligopoly**[19] and, in the extreme, like a **monopoly**.[20]
   5. Pricing in oligopoly and monopoly strongly favors sellers.
      a. In monopoly, only one firm makes the product consumers want, and that producer thereby gains control over pricing.
      b. In the more common situation of oligopoly, this control is incomplete, but nevertheless, usually provides producers with more control of pricing than is possible in perfect competition.
      c. In both instances, the firm usually increases its survival odds, begins to build competitive advantage, and earns a profit. The advantage in this case is the ability to improve process.
   6. We use the term **process enhancement** to refer to finding ways to reduce the cost of making otherwise comparable products, or to increase the quantity made for the same aggregate cost, or to otherwise increase the capability of the production system.
      a. The first two of these are usually also called **productivity (or efficiency) improvements.**
      b. Productivity enhancement is important for many reasons, which will be detailed later in the book. For now, though, we have briefly introduced a second means of escape from pure competition.

    c. So, when we think about the major players in this industry, one is an **entire firm** (Coca-Cola) while the other is not the entire firm, but just the **division** that makes and sells beverages (actually, two divisions in this particular case, PepsiCo Beverages North America and PepsiCo International).

B. Formal classification systems: The **federal** perspective.

  1. For various reasons, the federal government has developed systems to classify firms into one or more industries.

    a. The standard system for many years was called the Standard Industrial Classification (SIC) system. In 1997, the North American Industrial Classification System (NAICS) officially replaced the SIC system.

    b. However, the Security and Exchange Commission (and probably other Federal agencies also) still uses the SIC system, so it hasn't vanished.[1]

  2. For many purposes, the SIC/NAICS codes are useful. For example, you may want to visit www.census.gov/epcd/www/sic.html for a listing of useful data sets available on-line from the US Census Bureau.

  3. However, the term tends to be used differently in practice.

C. The **substitutability** approach to identifying industries.

  1. The idea here is that firms in the same industry are likely to demonstrate demand-side substitutability or supply-side substitutability or both. What's that mean?

    a. **Demand-side substitutability** refers to the possibility of customers switching between suppliers.

      (1) For example, a buyer of a retail checking account could buy from PNC, or Citibank, or a large number of other banks.

      (2) Similarly, you may prefer Burger King, but very similar products are also offered by McDonald's and Wendy's, among others.

    b. **Supply-side substitutability** refers the similarity of technologies used by producers.

      (1) For example, currently, Campbell's is a firm with lots of knowledge and experience turning tomatoes into prepared food. I don't think they make ketchup. Heinz does. Customers looking for ketchup won't find it at Campbell's. By the <u>demand-side definition</u>, Heinz is "in" the ketchup industry and Campbell's is not.

      (2) However, does Campbell's have the technology to make ketchup? Offhand, I don't know. But if they did, then under a supply-side definition, we would consider both firms in the same industry.

      (3) The technologies do not have to be identical for this to occur.

      (4) Also, obviously, just because the firm has the technology does not imply they actually make the product.

  2. OK, we have two possible definitions based on "substitutability." Let's make sure we understand how these differ (please refer to Table 3-1).

Table 3–1 Comparison of Demand- and Supply-Side

	Demand-side Substitutability	**Supply-side Substitutability**
Perspective	From buyer's perspective	From seller's perspective
Implications	What alternative firms exist from whom I (as a buyer) may purchase the product?	What other firms make OR have the ability to make the same product I (as a producer) make and sell?
Availability of critical information	Usually relatively easy to determine which producers make substitutable products.	Usually relatively difficult to determine which firms have the technology to make product that they currently are not making.

3. Which definition is better? **It depends on the question being asked**.
    a. From a seller's perspective, the supply-side approach considers <u>those players currently making the product</u> (obviously they have the technology) AND <u>also potential new players</u>. This may be important when the seller tries to estimate their future demand.
    b. From a buyer's perspective, the supply-side approach may not help much if you want the product today.
        (1) **If** you can delay your purchase, it may be useful because you believe that in, say a year, new sellers may emerge.
            (a) If so, you may have more choice of suppliers.
            (b) If the new player's product is more or less the same as the current one, then, prices may tend down.
            (c) If the new product has some new set of attributes, then you may find a product better suited to your interests.
        (2) However, **if you cannot or will not** delay your purchase (assume you're hungry right now and unwilling to wait a year for a new restaurant), then from the buyer's perspective, the demand-side approach has more appeal.
    c. Notice, demand-side substitutability generally provides a "narrower" definition of industry than does the supply-side approach.
4. Let's try an example. The product is an MBA degree. From the demand side definition, the "MBA industry" consists of those players you know to offer such a degree. But from the point of view of a graduate business school, the industry consists of those currently offering such a degree plus those likely to enter the market in the next year or two.

D. Personally I prefer the supply-side approach.
1. However, as noted in Table 3–1, the general public usually has more information about the demand-side than about the supply-side. <u>That is, outsiders to the firm usually have more and better information about the firm's products than about its technologies.</u>

---

2. In this course, we will use both approaches.
    a. Hence, if two firms are demand-side substitutable, we will consider them to be in the same industry. This is particularly useful from the buyer's perspective.
    b. If two firms are supply-side substitutable, we will also consider them to be in the same industry. This is particularly useful from the seller's perspective.
    c. Please realize this will produce some inconsistencies.

IV. Industry boundaries and related topics.

A. Industry boundaries.
1. Industries don't have exact boundaries, and hence they can often be defined at different "levels" depending on the question we wish to ask.
2. For example, think about the entertainment industry.
    a. While we could certainly consider this an important industry for some kinds of questions, a little thinking suggests that it consists of wildly different kinds of entertainment, from professional sports to movies to ballet to rock concerts.
    b. Indeed, each one of these could be thought of as an industry, for example, professional sports. But professional sport consists of wildly different sports from NASCAR to basketball to snowboarding to bullfighting. And any one of these could be thought of as an industry.
3. You get the idea. You have to make the call where to draw the boundaries and usually this depends on the questions you want to address.[2]

B. Rivals.
1. Earlier, we defined competitors as other players on the same side of the transaction space as you in any particular market in which you participate.

2. **Rivals are a special type of competitor, namely, those competitors that sell what you sell.**
   a. As just discussed, these rivals may "look" different depending on how the industry is defined.
   b. These rivals could be entire firms or divisions of firms.
   c. And linking all this to another idea from earlier in this chapter, firms that participate in multiple industries may do this by having one division in one industry and a second division in a different industry.

C. Which leads to an interesting question, namely, why would a firm ever participate in more than one industry? Or, maybe to ask the same question a different way, is there any upper limit to the number of industries in which a firm could participate?

   1. First observation: This is a complex topic, and the discussion here is basic.
   2. Second observation: We know that some firms participate in only one business area, while other participate in more than one (remember Coca-Cola and PepsiCo?).
      a. If one approach were uniformly better than the other, we may expect to see all firms "do something similar," that is, all be in just one business or all be in more than one business.
      b. However, in practice some firms are in just one or two businesses, while others are in dozens (or more).
      c. This suggests that there must be some underlying tradeoff.
   3. For our purposes, this tradeoff is between the **benefits of focus** (doing one business exceedingly well) and the **avoidance of risk**.
      a. Quick idea—If your firm is in one business, then you may do that very well, but something outside of your control may occur to disrupt that business and then the firm has no "fallback."
      b. One way to think of a fallback is to be in a second business. But if your firm does two things, it is difficult to do both equally well, so you lose some of the benefit of focus. Firms that are in more than one business area are called **diversified**. Firms in one business are called **focused**.
      c. Which raises the next question: The second business could be in same or a closely related industry to the first OR the second business could be in a totally different industry. If it's the former, then there may be some "spill-over" effects of focus—that is, knowledge of how to do business #1 well also helps you do business #2 well. However, when the businesses are related, than the risk of failure in business #1 may be similar (or identical) to risks that affect business #2. If it's the latter, then it is less likely for there to be any spillover effects, but things that may kill one business may have minimal effects on the other.
      d. If a firm is diversified into related businesses, we use the phrase **related diversification**. If the multiple businesses are not related, we call it **unrelated diversification**.
      e. What does all this suggest? A firm in one business gets the maximum impact of focus, but also the greatest risk exposure. A firm in many unrelated areas may reduce its risk exposure, but loses the benefits of focus. An intermediate position occurs when firms are in multiple related businesses.
   4. **In practice, then, all firms need decide to "where" on this tradeoff frontier they believe best balances focus and risk.**

V. Industry analysis—basic ideas.

   A. **Industry analysis** is the process of systematically analyzing an industry.
   B. Porter's five-forces model.
      1. In his 1980 book, Michael Porter presented what has become the standard approach to industry analysis.[3] While his model has many flaws, it's an excellent framework for us to consider here, as it is probably the best known system of industry analysis. Other methods are also available.
      2. The general question Porter was trying to answer was "<u>what are the basic factors that affect the profitability (or attractiveness) of an industry</u>?"
         a. His immediate answer was "The competitive situation in the industry."
         b. Which leads to the question: "What affects the competitive situation in an industry?" (Assuming that greater competition usually lowers prices and hence reduces industry profitability.)

    c. He then identifies five forces that affect the competitive situation:

      (1) Competition among the rivals currently selling more or less similar products (what Porter calls **competition from rivals**).

      (2) Competition from other players that <u>could</u> sell more or less similar products (**competition from new entrants**).

      (3) Competition from players that sell substitute products (what Porter calls **competition from substitutes**).

      (4) The **relative power of customers**.

      (5) The **relative power of suppliers**.

    d. These are usually organized into a diagram provided in Figure 3-1.

3. Thinking about how each of the five forces affects industry competition.

    a. Competition from rivals:

      (1) All other things equal, when there are many rivals and each is small (similar to what we see in perfect competition), the greater the degree of competition we would expect among these rivals.

      (2) This is exacerbated if . . .

        (a) demand in the industry were **shrinking or flat or only growing very slowly** (say, only 1 to 2 percent a year);

        (b) the industry has **excess capacity** (this occurs when total industry capacity exceeds total industry demand), <u>especially when shutting down the excess capacity is expensive</u>; and/or

        (c) there are high **exit costs** (exit costs are the unrecoverable costs of completely leaving the industry).

      (3) <u>Bottom line</u>: We expect competition among rivals is greater when . . .

        (a) there are many small producers,

        (b) there is weak or negative growth in demand,

        (c) there is excess capacity that is expensive to shut down, and

        (d) there are high exit costs.

<u>All things equal, greater competition would be expected to reduce the profitability (or attractiveness) of the industry.</u>

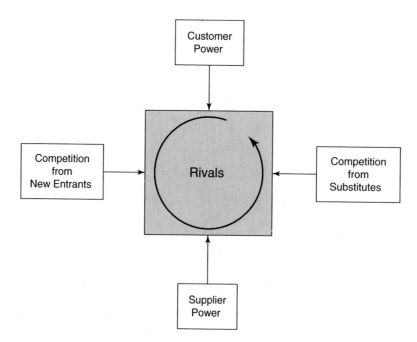

Figure 3–1 Porter's Five–Forces Model

b. Competition from new entrants:
  (1) At issue here is the relative ease of entering the industry.
  (2) Various **entry barriers** can be identified, which tend to inhibit the ease of entering the industry, including
      (a) Can the firm obtain the needed technology?
      (b) How much does it cost to enter?
      (c) Are there **economies of scale**? (That is, are there major unit cost advantages to a big entry rather than a small entry which will raise the entry costs?)
      (d) Do existing current customers exhibit substantial **brand loyalty** to the existing products?
  (3) For example, if it is expensive to enter and there are substantial economies of scale and existing customers are brand loyal and it is difficult to obtain the needed technologies, then we say entry barriers are very high. Conversely, if entry is not expensive, there are no scale economies, current customers seem willing to try new direct alternatives, and the needed technology is readily available, then we say entry barriers are very low.
  (4) <u>Other things equal, if entry barriers are low, than we would expect lower levels of profitability in the industry</u>.
      (a) Why?
      (b) All things equal, low entry barriers tend to induce new players to enter with products virtually identical to yours. (You may have seen this in micro-economics as the assumption of "no costs to enter" when you discussed perfect competition.) For example, new pizza shops open every day.
      (c) If there are many new entrants, rivalry among players—existing and new—tends to increase as the customers now have more choices.
        • To the degree to which industry competition is on price, price will tend downward, decreasing industry profitability.
        • Also, existing players may try to reduce price as a means of reducing the incentives for yet more players to enter, again reducing industry profitability.
c. Competition from substitutes:
  (1) Let's try an example first. Let's say you drive to school. Possible substitute forms of transportation include buses, walking, biking, skateboards, and so on.
  (2) You are likely to substitute one of the other transportation modes . . .
      (a) to the degree to which you are predisposed to switch and
      (b) to the degree to which price-performance characteristics of the alternative modes of travel are advantageous.
  (3) Example: You are a Pitt student. If you travel in Allegheny County, you pay nothing incremental over student fees to take the bus. If it's too far to walk and you have no car (or bike, etc.), then this is a no-brainer. Indeed, even if you have a car, the sheer cost of driving and parking and tickets may tilt you to take the bus.
  (4) <u>Other things equal, if competition from substitutes is high, then we would expect lower levels of profitability in the industry</u>.
      (a) Why?
      (b) Substitutes that are price-performance attractive tend to reduce price asked by many or all of the rivals.
      (c) The result is lower industry profitability.
d. Relative customer power.
  (1) In general, buyers are price sensitive, suggesting they shop, at least in part, on price. The greater the price sensitivity, the greater the pressure on the rivals to reduce price to attract buyers, and the lower the profitability of the industry.
  (2) However, at least two things work "in the other direction." The first is **brand loyalty**. If buyers are brand loyal, then they tend to restrict their purchases to those of a particular brand. If so, then at least some of the rivals can increase price, increasing the profitability of the industry.

(3) The second are **switching costs**. The idea here is if there are significant costs to the buyer associated with switching from one rival to another, then we say switching costs are high. If switching costs are high, the buyer is essentially stuck, and cannot switch to another seller without incurring additional costs. These costs could be monetary (cancellation fees with cell phone providers) or in non-monetary form (you transfer from one school to another, and you lose a semester).

(4) If the buyers have lots of information about prices and products of the suppliers, and if buyer can switch between suppliers at little or no cost, and if buyers are not brand loyal, then customer power is high. If buyers have little information, have high switching costs, and are brand loyal, then customer power is low.

(5) All things equal, if customer power is low, then we would expect higher levels of industry profitability. Conversely, if customer power is high, we expect lower levels of industry profitability.

e. Relative supplier power.

(1) Good example here: Assume you are a PC manufacturer. How many suppliers can provide high quality CPUs or operating systems? Very few. How much power do Intel and Microsoft have over PC makers? A lot. This is particularly true if switching to alternative suppliers is difficult or very costly.

(2) All things equal, if supplier power is low, then we would expect higher levels of industry profitability. Conversely, if supplier power is high, we expect lower levels of industry profitability.

VI. Industry analysis—a brief example.

A. Remember, what we are trying to do with an industry analysis.

1. Our main interest is to understand those elements of the environment that may affect **industry profitability**.

2. Please note carefully.

a. If industry profitability is high, that industry is a more attractive arena for all rivals, on average.

b. However, whether a particular firm in the industry is profitable or not is only partly dependent on industry attractiveness. By itself, industry analysis tells us nothing about the profitability of a particular rival. We'll address that shortly.

B. This example considers the airline industry as it existed more or less in 2002.

1. We start by determining the industry boundaries.

2. We know from material above that setting industries boundaries is a judgment call that depends on the question we want to address. Let's say our specific interest is "How attractive is the regularly scheduled domestic airline passenger industry?"

3. Right away, this excludes charter flights (not regularly scheduled), non-U.S. airlines (not domestic), private planes (not regularly scheduled), and so on.

4. Given these boundaries, our next task is to identify the rivals.

a. The largest three players in 2002 were American, Delta, and United.

b. Others included Continental, US Airways, Southwest, Northwest, etc.

c. Exactly how many players to include is often an issue. In general you want to include all players if the total number is small, or if the number is large, all of the largest players.

C. Next we consider the competition among rivals.

1. The first issue is the number and size of players. Some homework suggests a relatively small number of players and some serious differences in size. This looks more like an oligopoly than say a perfect competition.[4] Hence, our initial sense is there is at least some theoretical reason to believe that industry profitability could be significant.

2. The next issue is demand. Again some homework would suggest that demand was decreasing due to a shrinking economy (think dot com melt down) even before 9/11, and then the tragedy caused

demand to shrink more quickly. Combining this with issue one above suggests that while some opportunity may exist in theory for nice industry profitability, sluggish demand may reduce it.

3. The third issue is capacity. The industry had some excess capacity even before demand started sliding, but after the slide began, it had increasing amounts of overcapacity (i.e., many more seats than could be filled). Again, the original rosy picture is getting bleaker.

4. The next issue is the cost of exit (shutting down supply). Some homework would suggest this was very expensive, as the firms were committed to existing aircraft (either because they were owned and being paid off or because they were leased and the firms couldn't easily get out of the leases) and landing slots, among other possibilities.

5. Finally, complete exit from the industry would be massively expensive.

6. Bottom line: Putting all these things together suggests significant competition among rivals, most probably depressing price and industry attractiveness.

D. <u>Next we consider competition from new entrants</u>.
1. While the costs of entry are significant and there are many entry barriers, we certainly have seen some new entrants in the recent past (e.g. Jet Blue).

2. Most, however, fail except in specialized markets. Moreover, with serious demand erosion, we didn't see much new entry during this period.

3. This tends to maintain or increase industry attractiveness.

E. <u>Next is competition from substitutes</u>.
1. Some homework would convince you that auto travel (and to some degree, train and bus travel) became more attractive during this period of time for short and mid-range travel.

2. This contributes to lower industry profitability.

F. <u>Relative power of suppliers</u>.
1. Suppliers to this industry include those providing fuel, the labor market, plane manufacturers, and gates (the landing slots at airports).

2. Since overcapacity existed, the plane manufacturers had relatively low power over the airlines. Similarly, the relative power of labor was decreasing. Fuel, though less expensive than now, still had reasonable power.

3. Bottom line: Not much erosion of attractiveness from supplier power.

G. <u>Relative power of customers</u>.
1. The combination of excess capacity and reduced demand provided lots of opportunity for those who were flying to shop on price. Another issue here was the increasing use of the web as a means to buy tickets and comparison shop, which also shifted power to customers.

2. Also brand loyalty rapidly vaporized, and switching costs are negligent.

3. Another tick toward unattractive.

H. Bottom line: Putting all of this together is complex, as you need to consider the relative strength of these forces. My knowledge suggests a seriously unattractive industry. Note, this would not have been the outcome of the analysis even three to four years earlier. Any wonder why we saw several bankruptcies by 2005?

I. Given all this, we may expect that things hit the traditionally priced firms hardest, and that the discount guys may have even benefited. And this was exactly true—Southwest, for example, did quite well, while the traditional guys didn't. There is a lot more that we can do with this. There are also many weaknesses in this type of analysis. But it's still a useful way to think about an industry.

J. Before we leave this conversation, let's recall Professor Porter's basic question: "What are the factors that affect the competitiveness (and hence, the profitability) of an industry?"
1. Five such factors were identified and then applied to the domestic airline industry.

2. We concluded that, in 2002, it's <u>not</u> an attractive industry. The importance of the analysis emerges from the implications (e.g., how attractive is the industry), **not** from the sheer description of the various forces.

3. **Important point**: <u>Saying industry profitability is low does not imply that all firms in the industry will suffer</u>. Indeed, in the airline industry, a few firms, such as Southwest, have been quite successful.

4. Why this is so is our next topic.

VII. Industry attractiveness, unique competitive advantages, and the firm's economic performance.

  A. A quick summary before we begin the new ideas.

    1. Firms conduct transactions with players in the environment. The environment is complex and, in theory, firms must monitor the environment extensively in an attempt to understand "what's happening out there." Markets are the specific arenas within which transactions occur. In theory, monitoring the environment implies monitoring all aspects of the environment that may affect all these various markets.

    2. Exhaustive monitoring is expensive, time consuming, difficult, and probably impossible. Hence, <u>we can view the Porter model as focusing our attention on the relevant environment</u> as defined by the industry in which the firm participates. This led us to consider rivals, suppliers, customers, potential new entrants, and substitutes.

    3. While useful, the Porter model has many problems.

      a. It often misses important issues. For example, it does not directly concern itself directly with macro-economic phenomena or technology.

      b. Other problems (not discussed above) include . . .

        (1) little or no concern with the dynamics of industry (it really doesn't tell us how an industry "got" to its current level of attractiveness or where it may be going—in this sense the model is cross-sectional);

        (2) little or no direct concern with what I earlier called regulatory mechanisms; and

        (3) the entire system doesn't work well with newly developing industries (because it is very difficult to identify various players).

      c. Also, as it turns out, some of the model's propositions have not received robust empirical support.[5]

    4. Nevertheless, for our purposes at this point, it's quite useful.

  B. OK, now the new stuff. Basically, what I'll do in this section is to sketch out an approach to why firms like Aldi and Southwest Airlines can be highly profitable even though their industries are not very attractive. I'll start with two propositions:

    1. **A firm's potential economic performance is dependent on industry attractiveness AND the firm's unique competitive advantages to exploit the industry situation it finds.**

    2. **A firm's unique competitive advantages are dependent on its resources, its history, and the past choices made by its dominant coalition.**

  C. Proposition 1 allows us to simplify the world as noted in Table 3-2.

    1. If the industry is attractive and the firm possesses unique competitive advantages capable of exploiting the industry situation, the firm has the potential for a high level of economic performance.

    2. If the industry is attractive but the firm does not possess unique competitive advantages, the firm has a lower potential.

      a. Note, however, if the industry is particularly attractive, the firm may still "be successful" (in terms of being able to make reasonable profits). It may also fail.

      b. Often we see such firms make investments to build unique competitive advantages (why?).

      c. However, sometimes we observe all such firms reduce investments in seeking unique competitive advantages and substitute explicit or implicit collusion[6] (why?).

    3. If the industry is unattractive, but the firm has unique competitive advantages, then it should have higher potential economic performance than those in the industry without these advantages. However, if the industry is particularly unattractive, even this firm may fail.

      a. There may be significant incentives in this kind of industry for those firms that have unique competitive advantages to continue to improve these advantages, if industry unattractiveness is not too severe.

      b. Given our analysis of the airline industry, this is the situation faced by Southwest.

      c. In general, if find a weak industry with a strong rival (e.g., Southwest in the airline industry), you should expect that there is something quite special about how the firm does business.

    4. If the industry is unattractive and the firm has no unique competitive advantages, then we would expect one of several possible outcomes:

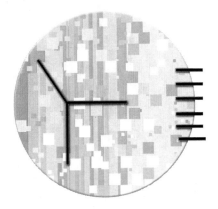

Active Practice

My strong suggestion is that you:

- Tear out the next few perforated pages from this section
- Close the book
- Answer the questions posed without looking at the book
- Please bring to class

Active Practice for Chapter 3: Industries

Assume you have a summer internship with a firm that is considering distribution of specialized medical reports and updates via e-reader devices such as Kindle and other digital media machines. As one of many preliminary steps, they ask you to conduct a Porter-type Industry Analysis of these devices. Below, please outline how you would go about doing this.

Please turn to the next page.

What problems do you expect to encounter?

If We Could Make a Blue Tomato, Would Anyone Buy It?

> "... a sale cannot be achieved if only the seller understands the value of the merchandise."[1]
>
> A. Morita

I. Teaser.
   A. Tomatoes come in many sizes, shapes, and colors (red, green, and yellow). Assume we could grow a nice, juicy, tasty blue tomato. Would you buy it?
   B. Posing this question to students generates three different types of answers: No, maybe, yes. About 50 to 60 percent of a typical class says "No." When asked, "Why not?" standard replies include:
      1. I hate all tomatoes.
      2. Sounds yucky (or stronger descriptors).
      3. I don't usually like new food things.
   C. Asking those who said yes "Why?" you hear:
      1. I like to be different.
      2. Sounds cool.
      3. It'll gross people out.
   D. Blue tomatoes sound strange, but most things we use all the time once didn't exist. Someone invented or developed them and then "brought them to the market." When they came to the market, some of us tried them and some didn't. Our concern in this lecture is with the general idea of marketing and "bringing new things to market"—and why we see lots of new things brought to the market every day—and why some succeed and others fail.[2]
   E. By the way, would you try a blue tomato?

II. Some basic ideas.
   A. Marketing.
      1. In the most basic sense, marketing concerns the methods by which each party to a transaction attempts to influence certain behavior of other parties to the transaction.
      2. We'll spend considerable effort below getting a handle on marketing, but first we need to address several preliminary issues, including revisiting transactions, exchange, and products, and developing the ideas of brand, value, and something called the "relationship marketing orientation."

B. Transaction and exchange.

 1. In Chapter 2, we introduced the concept of a transaction as an exchange of goods and services among buyers and sellers perhaps assisted by third parties.

 2. At that time, we noted that transactions are characterized in many ways (legal or not, purchase or barter, spot or future, domestic or international, market or transfer, and by type of primary good or service being exchanged).

 3. In addition to these characteristics, several conditions must exist for a transaction to occur.

   a. There must be at least two parties.

   b. Each party must have something that is of value to the other party.

   c. Each party can freely accept or reject the exchange.

   d. Each party is capable of communicating with the other party either directly or through an intermediary.

   e. Each party is capable of delivering the good or service to the other party or of making the good or service available for delivery.

   f. Each party believes it is appropriate or desirable to deal with the other party.

 4. Exchange generally occurs as a means to increase the benefit (or utility) of all parties to the transaction.

   a. That is, generally all parties believe they will be "better off" after the transaction has occurred. (**Please note**: Unless otherwise stated, we'll assume here that all transactions are spot—therefore, unless otherwise noted, when you see something like "striking a transaction," please read it to mean "striking and consummating a transaction." Also, "all parties" pertains to not just buyers and sellers, but also to third parties).

   b. For example, if I wish to sell my labor and your firm has need for an employee with my skills, we may strike a deal so that I exchange my labor for salary. Presumably, I am better off with the job (and the salary, etc) than with no job, and you are better off with my labor than without it.

   c. Please note:

     (1) Being "better off" after the transaction occurs does <u>not</u> mean optimally better off. There may have been a better job for me out there or a better employee for you. Apparently, however, at the point of striking the transaction, each of us was sufficiently better to stop searching for alternatives.

     (2) While I may believe I'll be "better off" after the transaction does not guarantee that I will actually be "better off."

 5. In brief, a <u>bona fide</u> transaction is a freely entered (uncoerced) actual exchange among parties that have some form of communication and produces benefits to all parties, typically assisted by third parties (who also expect to benefit).

C. Products.

 1. People have needs and wants, many of which can be satisfied by products. <u>A **product** is an offering by one party to a transaction that can satisfy a need of the other party to the transaction.</u>

 2. The traditional literature identifies two types of products: goods and services. The key difference between goods and services is the degree to which the product is tangible: services are the more "intangible" products, while goods are the more "tangible."

 3. Although the "product as goods and services" terminology is still commonly used, in practice today we often distinguish many different types of products:

   a. **Goods** are physical (or tangible) and usually transportable offerings. Examples range from clothes to huge industrial machines.

   b. **Services** are offerings that are intangible and usually created at the same time as they are provided. Examples include a haircut, banking, legal advice, medical treatment, and transportation.

     (1) Most goods have a service component, but many services have no discernable goods component.

     (2) For example, a new car is a good, but your choice of which to purchase may be influenced by which dealership provides better maintenance and repair services. On the other hand, education is a service for which it is difficult to identify a goods component.

   c. **Information** is an offering of structured sets of data and other material, such as magazines, newspapers, and web sites.

d. **Experiences** are offerings constructed of multiple goods and services organized to create and provide a particular "feel." Examples include a Disneyland "experience" or a vacation cruise "experience."

e. **Events** are offerings of specific time-based occurrences, such as a concert or a graduation ceremony, often constructed of a combination of services and goods (e.g., a concert at which you listen to the music and can buy CDs).

f. **Places** are offerings of physical locations or the location's facilities and amenities. Examples include demonstrating what a great place Lake Como is for a vacation, the advantages of locating your firm in Ireland, or shooting your movie in Pittsburgh.

g. **Properties** are the offerings of the rights of ownership to real (physical, but unmovable) or intellectual (creative) property. Examples include houses (real property) and patents (intellectual property).

h. **Persons** are the offerings of the rights to the time and activities of an individual, such as may be done by an agent representing a celebrity.

i. **Organizations** are offerings of the benefits of joining a specific firm, association, or institution. Best example here is how universities and clubs present themselves to you as a great place for students.

j. **Ideas** are the offerings of concepts, opinions, or principles. Examples include such things as academic freedom or libertarianism.

k. You may think these distinctions trivial or silly, and perhaps they are. However, as a practical matter, we have seen enormous expansion in the past decade or so of the traditional concept of product as simply good or service. For an interesting example, please check out the marketing of experiences as gifts offered by one firm (www.excitations.com).

4. Many products have aspects of more than one of these specific types.

D. Brand.

1. We'll have much more to say about the concept of brand in a short while.

2. In the most general sense, a brand is just an identifier. In practice we can think of a **brand** as identifying a product from a known source.

a. A brand name such as McDonald's or Harvard or Mercedes carries many **associations** in the minds of people. McDonalds may convey fast food, familiarity, and/or high fat content.

b. Associations are of three types:

(1) beliefs (organized bits of knowledge—"Rolex is expensive"),

(2) attitudes (positive or negative emotions—"I like Juicy Couture"),

(3) predispositions to act ("I search for Jimmy Choo shoes").

c. Firms invest considerable resources to create positive brand images (i.e., strong positive associations), and most work hard to avoid or counteract anything that would tarnish a positive image.

E. Value, satisfaction, and rationality.

1. Above, we noted that all parties expect to feel "better off" after consummating the transaction.

2. Presumably, if you feel "better off" (as buyer, seller, or third party), you should experience some level of satisfaction.

a. Clearly, post transaction experience may condition satisfaction, up or down.

b. For example, as a seller, your satisfaction may soar if the buyer makes a second purchase or plummet if the buyer's check bounces.

3. But we all know that satisfaction comes in many degrees—enter the concept of value.

a. Value is "how much" one party gets relative to what that party gives in order to strike and consummate the transaction.

b. Example 1: Assume you drop $6 for lunch at new restaurant. Imagine the meal was brilliant—you think "good value" relative to, say, paying $5 at McD's.[3]

c. Example 2: The New York Times and The Wall Street Journal both have weekly wine columns. In addition to reviews and normal prices, usually one wine is identified as "best" and one as the "best buy." Most of the time they are different wines—one provides the greatest satisfaction (of that lot) while the other delivers the best satisfaction for the price. "Value purchase" and "value choice" are synonyms for "best buy."

    d. Please note the following carefully:

      (1) Some parties are particularly sensitive to value, that is they tend to seek transactions that produce the greatest satisfaction for the price (we'll call them "value buyers").

      (2) Some parties are particularly sensitive to price alone, that is they seek transactions that are lowest price, as long as the transaction reaches some minimum level of satisfaction (we'll call them "price buyers").

      (3) Some parties are particularly sensitive to satisfaction alone, that is they seek transactions that provide the greatest satisfaction as long as some budget constraint is not exceeded (we'll call them "status buyers").

    e. We may speculate that in a period of recession (such as much of the past twenty-four months) status buyers become more "value sensitive" And many buyers become increasingly price sensitive.

  4. Finally, we'll assume parties to a transaction are rational in the sense of seeking and striking transactions that they believe achieve a consistent criterion from among the transactions they believe available to them.

    a. <u>Criterion</u>. As we have just observed, the criterion may vary as some parties are relatively more sensitive to price, to value, or to status.

    b. <u>Consistent</u>. We will assume that for any particular class of transactions, parties are consistent in terms of these sensitivities, although clearly this could vary over products or particular situations. For example, I may be price sensitive for shoes, value sensitive for sweaters, and status sensitive special occasion restaurant meals.

    c. <u>Transactions parties believe available</u>.

      (1) In theory, we assume buyers know all sellers and hence can search all sellers.

      (2) In practice buyers usually do not know all sellers and hence, they usually search only among a subset of all sellers.[4]

F. Channels.

  1. Channels are complex links among parties to transactions. Typically, we can identify two kinds: marketing channels and supply channels.

  2. **Supply channels** are an entire set of links that trace from raw material suppliers to end-users (or any part of the overall chain of links), where the end user is the actual user of the product. If we think of the burger you buy at Burger King, the supply chain is the entire set of links from you back to cattle raisers, paper producers, and so on.

  3. **Marketing channels** refer to the shorter set of links between potential sellers and buyers at any point in the entire supply chain. Continuing the above example, we can talk about the marketing channels that link Burger King to you or that link a particular paper supplier to BK. There are several types of marketing channels:

    a. **Communication channels** provide information that could range from advertising to inquiries about products via the Internet.

    b. **Distribution channels** display and deliver product.

    c. **Selling channels** effect transactions. In the Burger King example above, selling channels may include regular walk-up, drive-through, and who knows maybe internet or fax ordering.

G. Relationship marketing orientation.

  1. The idea here is "what drives" the products made by the firm?

    a. There are many possibilities:

      (1) Opportunity: Make whatever is the "new, hot stuff."

      (2) Technology: Make what we know best how to make.

      (3) Production: Make what we can best make with existing equipment.

      (4) Sales: Make what we know best how to sell.

      (5) Customer: Make what our target market most wants.

    b. Each of these is used by some firms.

2. <u>The dominant view today is to focus on the customer</u>, particularly those customers with whom our firm wishes to develop a long term relationship.
   a. Implementing this by focusing the firm's activities on satisfying our target customers is known as the **relationship marketing orientation.** This orientation concerns creating, communicating, and delivering more value to our target customer over the long haul than could be obtained from a rival.
   b. The actual set of activities to accomplish this end is often called **customer relationship marketing** or **CRM.**

3. This approach may seem obvious. However, this is relatively new (perhaps ten to twenty years or so, depending on the industry). Indeed, some authors have proposed a subtle shift over time from a production to a sales to a relationship marketing orientation.[5]

4. While easy to discuss, it's hard to do. Two books discussing the difficulty of doing this at Xerox are <u>Prophets in the Dark</u>[6] and <u>The Force</u>.[7] The former is written from a top management perspective and the latter from a sales team's view. If you are interested in marketing, read one or both of them.

III. OK, so what's "marketing"? How does it differ from "a market"?
   A. In Chapter 2, we defined a market as an arena within which transactions occur.
      1. The American Marketing Association defines "**marketing**" as the *"process of planning and executing conception, pricing, promotion and distribution of ideas, goods, and services to create exchanges that satisfy individual and organizational goals."* [8] A **market** is the arena within which the exchange occurs.
      2. This definition of marketing emphasizes two somewhat distinct ideas:
         a. Several **functions of marketing** are identified (e.g., conception, pricing, promotion, and distribution), and
         b. The **integrated goal of these functions** is identified (the creation of exchanges that satisfy individual and organizational goals—although it isn't really obvious in this definition whether these exchanges satisfy the seller, the buyer, or both).
      3. I should know better than to take exception with the American Marketing Association's definition of their professional field. However, I'd like you to consider an alternative view. Marketing can also be viewed as *"the process by which one party in a market attempts to increase the likelihood that they strike the transactions that they wish to strike."*
         a. The reason I market anything is to increase the number and/or value of transactions I can strike that are long term advantageous to me in all markets in which I participate.
         b. Two brief examples
            (1) Marketing is the process used by Nike to increase the likelihood that you buy their shoes instead of, say, a pair of Adidas.
            (2) However, marketing is also the process by which Nike increases the likelihood that you will accept their job offer rather than one you got from Adidas (assuming, of course, that you got job offers from both).
      4. Think for a second about these two examples. In what important way do they differ?
         a. In the first example, both Nike and Adidas are sellers (of shoes); in the second example, both are buyers (of your labor).
            (1) We usually think of the seller as the party doing the marketing—**but this is not always the case.**
            (2) The labor market provides a great example.
               (a) Buyers of labor (potential employers) market extensively via websites, job fairs, newspaper advertising, and so on.
               (b) Sellers of labor (you looking for a job) also marketing via resumes, contacts, and dressing appropriately for interviews.
               (3) We will use the phrase "seller marketing" or just "marketing" when the seller is doing the marketing, and "buyer marketing" when it's the buyer. Seller marketing is by far the better studied situation.

b. In the first example, the focus was on the finished goods market; in the second example, the focus was on the labor market.

   (1) We usually associate marketing with the finished goods market—**but this is not always the case**.

   (2) In general, marketing can and does occur in all markets, even if the basic concepts are most well developed for finished goods.

c. In the first example, only one party to the transaction was engaged in marketing; in the second example, both parties were probably engaged in marketing.

   (1) You were trying to influence both firms to hire you and both firms were trying to influence you accept their offer.

   (2) We usually think that only one party in a transaction "does the marketing," **but this is not always true**.

   (3) However, in the more typical case, only one party engages in significant marketing.

d. Finally, thinking only about the second example (the job situation), the "product" you were trying to market was a person (your time and talent), while the firm may have been trying to market an organization or maybe an experience. So, **in the same transaction, each party can be engaged in marketing a different product**. Only if there is overlap among these products would we expect to observe a transaction.

5. Returning to the main theme: Marketing can be viewed in two ways.

   a. #1: Marketing is the **integrated action of a specific set of functions** (such as conception and development of new products, product promotion, distribution, and pricing) that somehow affects what products are available and how you learn about products and the firms that make them.

   b. #2: Marketing is the process of **increasing the utility** of the transaction in a market so that the transaction is more likely to occur than some alternative transaction.

B. Marketing as utility creation.

1. What's utility?

   a. Working definition: "the power of a product to satisfy a need."

   b. Utility is also a measure of the degree to which the need is satisfied.

2. Four types of utility.

   a. The product has the attributes to satisfy the need (**form utility**).

   b. The product is available in the place desired (**place utility**).

   c. The product is available at the time desired (**time utility**).

   d. The product transaction is as desired (**possession utility**).

3. All this sounds pretty theoretical—but it's really very practical. Think of it this way. If you are buying a shirt, you are more likely to buy one that . . .

   a. is the size, style, and color you desire (form utility),

   b. is in a store at which you prefer to shop (place utility),

   c. is in the store when you are in the mood to buy (time utility), and

   d. can be bought with, say, cash, check, or plastic (possession utility).

4. That is, all things equal, you are more likely to buy the product that has greater utility for you as opposed to alternatives.

   a. Using terminology introduced above, this is another way of saying that we assume the buyer is a rational party, choosing from among a set of known alternatives that one which best satisfies his/her interests.

   b. However, not all products are likely to be in your set of alternatives. As suggested above, when you buy a shirt, you don't choose from all shirts in the world, just from those that are in the set of known alternatives. As you may recall from the earlier discussion, in theory, the buyer knows all sellers, but in practice this simply isn't true.

   c. Hence, there may be some other product, not in your set of alternatives, which would better satisfy your interests. However, perhaps . . .

        (1) you can't find it, or

        (2) you need to make a choice now, or

        (3) you decide the costs of additional search aren't "worth it" or

        (4) you believe it is outside of your budget constraint.

   d. This is an important idea, so a few more comments are useful.

        (1) When you as a customer strike a transaction, we assume you have choice among alternatives.

        (2) Generally, you choose that alternative you believe will produce the best value or the greatest absolute benefit or the lowest price (as discussed above).

        (3) However, this choice is usually constrained by such things as a lack of information or time, or by the cost of searching for more alternatives.

        (4) It may also be the case that you have developed a long-term vendor relationship that has provided sufficient benefit in the past that you don't even search.

   e. Finally, exactly how you decide which alternative in a given set will produce the greatest satisfaction can be a very complex process.

  5. Two final caveats:

   a. OK, please recall our discussion of marketing as increasing the likelihood of striking the transactions you wish to strike. From this perspective, "being good at marketing" (for a seller) means at least three things . . .

        (1) Increasing the likelihood that the buyer's set of alternatives includes my firm and my firm's product (if not, it won't even be considered).

        (2) If it's not in the set of alternatives, increasing the likelihood that the buyer can find it quickly and/or at minimal search cost.

        (3) If it is in the set of alternatives, increasing the likelihood that it will be chosen.

   b. The above is written from the seller's perspective. The same case can be made for any party to the transaction (seller, buyer, or third party).

C. Marketing as different functions.

  1. Marketing affects utility via the specific activities of various marketing functions.

  2. There are many ways to catalog the various marketing functions. The following works well for our needs.

   a. **Product-related functions**:

        (1) Market research, which helps identify what elements may provide additional utility to a market segment.

        (2) Product development, or developing prototypes of the product.

        (3) Product standardization, or identifying and perhaps "forcing" product standards.

   b. **Transaction related**:

        (1) Pricing, or determining how to price a particular product (covered in detail in Chapter 5).

        (2) Promoting, or increasing the knowledge among market actors about your products, their use, and your existence as a market player, and other communication channel activities (covered in detail in Chapter 6).

        (3) Selling, which is the actual activity of striking the transaction.

        (4) Buying, or the activities of acquiring product for sale (or raw material for production).

        (5) Financing, or assisting the purchaser to obtain the funds necessary to make the purchase.

        (6) Risk management, a broad set of activities involving managing the risks associated with striking certain transactions.

   c. **Distribution related**:

        (1) Distribution channel functions and management, which deal with the mechanics of moving product from manufacturer to the point of sale and sometimes from the point of sale to the customer's location.

        (2) Supply chain management (some ideas re both of these are covered in Chapter 6).

  3. Many of you will major in marketing and nearly all of the above are possible career fields for you.

D. General observations regarding the above.
1. In general, marketing concepts apply to all markets and to all parties for the same basic reason: To increase the likelihood of a preferred transaction occurring. In practice, however, marketing concepts are most well developed for finished products markets and for use by sellers.
2. From the seller's perspective, marketing functions concern increasing the utility of the product in the eyes of the customer (or on reducing its cost while leaving the perception of utility unchanged, or both).
3. From the buyer's perspective, marketing functions focus on increasing the seller's perception of the utility of having the buyer as a customer.
4. Having made the point that any actor (seller, buyer, or third party) in any market can use marketing concepts, most of our remaining discussion of marketing will focus on sellers and finished goods markets.

IV. Product lines, product mix, and marketing mix.
A. Product lines.
1. **Product line** refers to a group of similar goods or services.
a. Product lines vary over time by **product extension** and **product refinement**.
(1) A product extension example follows: once there was only regular Coca-Cola, then a diet version (first Tab, then Diet Coke), then Caffeine-Free Coke, then Caffeine-Free Diet Coke; along the way Cherry Coke was added. Usually, product extension causes an increase in the number of products the firm sells.
(2) Product refinement usually involves improvement in the product (for example, improving the taste of a food product or increasing the speed of a PC) and removal of the older product from the market. Usually, product refinement changes the product but does not increase the number of products the firm markets (except, perhaps, during a phase-in period when both may be available in the market)
b. Product extensions and refinements often fail—example, McDonald's "Arch Deluxe" extension of a several years ago was a failure (as indicated by the fact that most of you guys never even heard of it).
c. Similarly, "New Coke" was a product refinement that failed a number of years ago. Consumers just didn't like it, and the firm quickly reintroduced the old formula.
2. Product lines are often "nested." GM has several product lines (cars are one; trucks are another) and within each, several models.
3. A related concept is **brand extension**. Product extension typically occurs within product line, while brand extension occurs when the firm applies an existing brand identifier to a new product in a new product line.
B. Product mix.
1. **Product mix** refers to the set of all products that the firm offers for sale within a given industry.
2. Product mix has two dimensions.
a. "Width," which is the number of product lines.
b. "Depth," which is the number of products within each line.
c. Please refer to Table 4-1 for an example involving General Mills.
C. Marketing mix.
1. **Marketing mix** refers to the overall set of decisions the firm uses to pursue its objectives.
2. The traditional approach here is to refer to the "4 P's."
a. **P**roduct: This would include decisions about form utility, product mix, packaging, other aspects of form utility, branding, and so on.
b. **P**rice: Decisions about pricing policy and other aspects of possession utility.
c. **P**romotion: Discussed briefly above as "increasing the knowledge among market actors about your products, their use, and your existence as a market player" or more specifically, advertising, public relations, sales promotion, direct marketing, and personal selling.
d. **P**lace: Decisions about place and time utility issues, and some aspects of distribution.
D. These are nested in the sense that marketing mix includes product mix and product line decisions, while product mix includes product line decisions.

  c. Others tend to have separate brand names for each or most products, for example, pharmaceutical makers call their stuff Nexium or Prozac.

 4. Often a firm that has used family branding has a difficult decision whether to continue using a family brand when they introduce a new product.

  a. This is particularly true if the firm targets the new product to a segment different than their traditional target market.

  b. A nice example here is Honda cars.

   (1) The traditional target market for Hondas was the low and middle price segments.

   (2) Quite a few years ago, they decided to try to penetrate the segment containing the 3-Series BMW.

    (a) Question: Should they call the new product "Honda" (such as a Honda X), or should they call the new product something unassociated with Honda?

    (b) What are the underlying issues?

     • Honda had, by that time, developed a reputation for well-engineered, lower-priced cars.

     • Would a well-engineered, higher-cost car benefit from this reputation (because of the decent engineering) or would it be hurt (because the traditional Honda customer focused on lower priced goods)?

    (c) They opted to develop a new brand—Acura.

   (3) Toyota (Lexus) and Nissan (Infiniti) made similar decisions at more or less the same time.

   (4) But not Daimler-Benz (the Mercedes guys)!

    (a) The situation at Daimler-Benz was a bit different.

    (b) In Europe, D-B introduced a new, low-end car (the A-class), which was really small and (in my opinion) rather funny looking.

    (c) D-B decided that the Mercedes name would appeal to low-end buyers, while not alienating traditional buyers.

 5. These examples raise several important issues.

  a. Brand names, when well developed, have many positive associations with strong implications to buyers.

   (1) They may convey important aspects of image.

   (2) They may convey important information about quality.

   (3) They may convey important information about a willingness to remain in the market.

   (4) They may convey important information about the firm's willingness to "stand behind" the product.

   (5) Many other associations can be identified

  b. Because of the image of the product produced by the brand name, buyers may be willing to . . .

   (1) purchase without as much "research,"

   (2) overlook certain negative things about the product, or

   (3) pay more for the product (as compared to other products targeted to the same segment).

  c. However, a strong brand may not impress different target markets or may upset existing buyers if used on products for different segments.

D. All this suggests why "brand" is important.

 1. Benefits include . . .

  a. increased and more rapid recognition,

  b. customer loyalty,

  c. the perception of higher quality,

  d. the perception of more or better features,

  e. customer willingness to pay higher prices, and

  f. the creation of possible entry barriers.

2. As noted earlier, brand associations, regardless of specifics in a particular case, can be of three general types:
   a. beliefs (organized bits of knowledge—"Toyotas are reliable"),
   b. attitudes (positive or negative emotions—"I like Juicy Couture"), or
   c. predispositions to act ("I search for the net for Jimmy Choo shoes").
3. Are there any negatives? Sure.
   a. Building a strong brand (or brand image) is expensive.
   b. Customers usually bear these costs in the form of higher price.
4. Sometimes customers rebel against these higher prices.
5. This has led to two interesting phenomena.
   a. The emergence of "discounted" branded items.
      (1) One form is "factory outlet" stores.
          (a) These stores, often operated by the manufacturer, sell branded goods at lower than standard branded prices.
          (b) Sometimes the goods sold in these shops are first-quality, current products. Often, though, these shops sell either discontinued products or "seconds." Seconds are products with some (usually) minor quality defects that do not affect performance or appearance.
      (2) The second are retailers who regularly sell first-quality product at regularly discounted prices. Obvious here is Walmart.
   b. Two other interesting outcomes of customer rebellion against higher prices for branded goods can be identified:
      (1) The development of "generic" brands.
          (a) Cigarette manufacturers discovered this many years ago and generic cigarettes became a major "thing."
          (b) We now see a similar phenomenon with generic cereals.
      (2) The growth in private labels—think "Value Line" and "Market District" from Giant Eagle.
6. An interesting example.
   a. For about seventy years, the largest U.S. retailer was Sears. Over time they sold almost exclusively store-branded products (e.g., the Craftsman line of tools and the Kenmore line of appliances).
   b. They serviced a wide swath of the U.S. public, but generally focused on the "middle-brow" customer. Prices tended to be a bit lower than national branded items, but they weren't really a "discount" shop.
   c. Sometime in the 1970s a new guy, Kmart, who focused on discounted national branded items, overtook them.
      (1) In the language of Chapter 2, Kmart introduced a new business model—and a very successful one.[11] Sears was no longer king of the hill and struggled to re-establish itself.
      (2) For what it's worth, Kmart's stay on top didn't last too long, and as you may suspect, the largest U.S. retailer today is Walmart.
   d. The big question during the seventies and eighties was "Should Sears stick with its traditional store brand approach or should they emphasize national brands or some combination?" Eventually, they shifted toward a hybrid model, advertising themselves as "Brand Central."
   e. Once this shift was made, the next big issue was should they compete primarily on discounted price?
      (1) For reasons that will become more apparent later in the course, they couldn't successfully price compete against Walmart.
      (2) So, they chose to sell a wide variety of both store and nationally branded products at low, but far from lowest prices. In the process, they lost many, many traditional customers.
   f. So, what to do?
      (1) For a long time it wasn't clear what they were doing. From 1993 to 1999, they pursued the "softer side of Sears" theme trying to win women back to a store that had become a place for men to shop for tools and automotive goods. After 1999, they pushed "the good life at a great price . . . guaranteed" theme, apparently trying to claim they were price competitive.

(2) In 2001, we saw another shift as Sears changed "its pitches to emphasize the variety of name-brand merchandise sold by its 860 stores rather than trying to compete on pricing with discounters like Walmart Stores and Target."[12]

(3) To complete the story, Kmart bought Sears in November, 2004.[13]

E. Brand equity.

1. Brands are valuable assets to firms. For example, what value would you place on the brand "Target"? (I don't know, but a lot.)

2. **Brand equity** refers to the total economic value of the brand to the firm.

   a. Much of the economic value incorporated in brand equity has little or no accounting value under U.S. accounting standards.

      (1) For example, the brand name itself can have enormous economic value, but this is generally not recognized in an accounting sense until the brand name is subject to a "market test," i.e., is sold.

      (2) On the other hand, if a firm today has use of a brand name as the result of a purchase of that name from its original owner, the brand . . .

         (a) produced an accounting return to seller and

         (b) has an accounting value to its current owner.

3. In general terms, brand equity tends to increase with . . .

   a. brand awareness (the degree to which buyers are familiar with the brand),

   b. brand loyalty (the degree of commitment buyers have to the brand),

   c. perceived quality and other positive brand associations, and

   d. other assets such as patents and trademarks.

4. Firms go to great lengths to protect their brands and trademarks.

   a. Sometimes brand names receive such wide scale use that they can no longer be used exclusively. Zipper, yo-yo, thermos, aspirin, kerosene, and escalator were once exclusively held brand names. Today, they are no longer protected.[14]

   b. Firms will often sue another firm if they think that the second firm infringes on one of its brands or trademarks.[15] For example, if I started up a shoe company and called my shoes Niike, do you think that Nike might sue me? You better believe it.

   c. A closely related phenomenon is the "knockoff." Walk the streets in any major city and you'll see street vendors selling "authentic" Ray-Bans or Louis Vuitton pocketbooks. Are they authentic?

      (1) Rarely. (And if authentic, usually hot.)

      (2) Does it matter?

         (a) Interesting question—probably a better question is "To whom does it matter?"

         (b) It matters to the manufacturer, whose brand mark, brand name, or trademarks may be used illegally or improperly.

         (c) Why does it matter to the manufacturer? It may reduce the manufacturer's legitimate sales and it may reduce brand equity (for example, if the product falls apart in two days, the customer may blame the presumed manufacturer).[16]

         (d) Having said that, many manufacturers do not pursue legal recourse either because of the cost or the relative difficulty of actually stopping the practice even if a suit is successful. Some manufacturers may even see it as having some positive sides ("imitation is the best form of flattery").

         (e) Does it matter to the customer? Hard question, as most customers of these products probably know they are knockoffs. They may actually prefer it, since it may convey the image of having the good at a very low price.

         (f) Does it matter to the street vendor? No, since they're making money on the transaction. Unless, of course, they run into legal problems.

   d. Is there really a difference between a knockoff and flat-out product piracy?

      (1) In a technical sense, probably not.

(2) But piracy, as a term, is used quite differently in most cases—piracy is the term used when the manufacturer aggressively attempts to stop the practice.

    (a) For example, software piracy is rampant on a global basis.[17] It exists in at least two forms:

      • firms that copy the software of other firms and then sell it, sometimes at steep discounts and sometimes at normal prices, as "original" to the general public; and

      • customers who copy software for their own use.

    (b) Both practices are generally illegal in the U.S. and many other countries.

e. A closely related issue emerges from various peer-to-peer web products such as introduced by the now defunct Napster in music.

    (1) Clearly, many people use these products.

    (2) But the underlying issues may be similar if such sharing . . .

      (a) reduces real purchase of the product,

      (b) reduces the earnings of the artist or author, or

      (c) is done in a way to circumvent normal commerce.

    (3) The legal concept here is not violation of a brand name, brand mark, or trademark—rather, it is concerned with a similar concept (copyrights) that allows an author or artist to protect creative products.

F. Bottom line:

1. Brand identifiers (brand names, brand marks, and trademarks) distinguish otherwise similar (or identical) offerings from each other.

2. Brands develop associations which convey important information to buyers, many of whom adjust their purchase behavior based on this information.

3. Brands may be developed and owned by either manufactures or retailers.[18]

4. Building strong brands can take considerable investment in time and money.

5. Good brands convey economic value to firms in the form of such things as increased loyalty by customers, even if not in accounting value.

6. Firms will usually act to protect their investments in these brands and in maintaining brand equity.

VII. Innovation, risk, and new product introduction.

A. First movers.

1. We know that firms differentiate product in the hopes of escaping the difficulty of competing in perfect competition.

2. If they properly develop a product that is uniquely suited to a market segment and <u>are the first to do so</u>, they may gain the benefits of being a monopolist in that segment, at least for some time.

3. A **first mover** is the first entrant in a new segment or the first entrant with significant product extension in an existing segment.

    a. Not all firms chose to product differentiate.

    b. Some stay with the generic product, seek process enhancements that increase productivity and decrease cost, and then lower the price of the generic product in an attempt to lure customers.

    c. Others stay with the generic product, but attempt to escape from the rigors of perfect competition by developing a new business model.

    d. Some firms may choose some combination of these three.

B. Even among those firms that do product differentiate <u>some prefer to follow a first mover strategy</u> while others are **followers**.

1. Why? Although the benefits that accrue to successful first movers are potentially great, being a first mover is risky, as there are no assurances of success.

2. Possible advantages of being a first mover (in no particular order):

    a. Intellectual property protection obtained by brand, trademark, or copyright (nice example here is "Walkman").

    b. Superior location (nice example here is the "location" of amazon.com).

    c. Reputation for innovation (e.g., Apple for consumer electronics).

   d. Distribution channel access/lock-up (the means of delivering product to the customer are limited, such as supermarket shelf space, and first movers may absorb all the "space" available for a class of products).
   e. Raw material access/lock-up. (When IBM entered the PC market, they wanted to buy chips from Motorola. Motorola probably would have wanted to sell chips to IBM, but Apple had already contracted for the bulk of their chip capacity.)
   f. Government/other license (the patent protection of a new drug).
   g. Could satiate market.
3. Possible disadvantages:
   a. The above advantages may not materialize.
   b. Costs of research and development are fully incurred by the first mover, while such costs are often lower for followers due to imitation and other factors.
   c. Product failure could occur even if there is adequate demand.
   d. Product timing could be off; someone else beats you to the market.
   e. Development costs may be so great that even if product "hits," you can't generate sufficient revenue to cover the product development.
4. <u>Bottom line</u>: Being a first mover is risky in the sense that the investment to bring the differentiated product to market are real and occur mostly before the first product is sold. Benefits, if any, come later and may be too small to recoup the investment. Hence, many firms choose to be followers, of which there are two types.

C. **Fast second movers** are followers poised to enter quickly if first movers seem to have a "hit."
   1. Advantages:
      a. Don't incur the full cost of development as you can learn from first movers.
      b. Don't have to educate the market about the benefits of the product.
      c. Don't have to enter if first mover fails; hence reducing your risk.
      d. Can use first mover experience to fine tune product or "leap frog" technology or product attributes.
   2. Disadvantages:
      a. May be shut out.
      b. Since you are late to enter, total potential volume may be lower than for first mover.
   3. Being a fast second mover is risky because the first mover's advantages make your entry difficult or impossible.
      a. Therefore, even though your costs may be lower, your potential benefits may also be smaller or non-existent.
      b. And, just as is true for the first mover, you spend the development money (even if lower) before you ever sell a product. Since there are no assurances that you can overcome the first mover's possible advantages, you could lose your entire investment.

D. **Slow second movers** enter after market characteristics are well understood.

E. So which is better?
   1. Will it surprise you if I say there is no easy answer? Instructive are some data summarized in Table 4-2, originally reported by David Teece.[19]
   2. What does Table 4-2 tell us?
      a. The answer to "which is better?" has no simple answers.
      b. Suffice here to say that if a first mover discovers a profitable market then what is critical is how well the first mover can defend its market position.
         (1) If the market is profitable, second movers **will** enter, perhaps in droves,
         (2) And each intends to overcome the natural advantages the first mover may have established.

F. Where do new product ideas come from?
   1. This is a much-studied question. I particularly like the work of Erik von Hippel[20] of MIT who begins by noting that fundamentally there are three sources of product innovation.
      a. Innovation developed completely by firm X.

Table 4-2   Comparing the Success of First and Second Movers

Product	First mover	Second Mover	Winner
Jet Airliner	DeHaviland	Boeing	Follower
Personal computer	Xerox	IBM	Follower*
Diet cola	R.C. Cola	Coca-Cola	Follower
Instant camera**	Polaroid	Kodak	Leader
Float glass	Pilkington	Corning	Leader
Disposable diaper	Proctor & Gamble	Kimberly-Clark	Leader
Social networking	Friendster	MySpace Facebook	Not Friendster (which most of you probably never heard of)

* And later, of course, Compaq (a follower of IBM)....And Dell, a follower to Compaq, has overtaken Compaq (while IBM exited the industry and HP bought Compaq) and today Dell is in trouble.

** Although, of course, instant photography of the Polaroid type has been completely overtaken by digital photography.

See D. Teece, The competitive challenge: Strategies for industrial innovation and renewal, Cambridge: Ballinger, 1987. The table is updated from material found on pp. 186–187.

   b. Innovation instigated by suppliers to firm X.
   c. Innovation instigated by customers of firm X.
 2. There are many examples of new product ideas from all three sources. Von Hippel's work, however, strongly suggests that customers, or at least certain customers, are more often the critical source of innovation.[21]
 3. What do I mean by certain customers?
   a. Just as firms differ in their propensity to be first movers, so do customers differ in their propensity to be **early adopters**.
   b. Customers who are early adopters appear to be important sources of new product ideas. Why?
     (1) They may provide ideas for emerging needs and technologies.
     (2) They may be willing to assist in the innovation process, either financially and by being the "testers" of the new product.
     (3) Since they are predisposed to adopt early, they provide an early source of revenue and provide an early estimate of the market's potential size, hence reducing some of the first mover's risk.
 4. Please recall our earlier discussion of the "relationship marketing orientation."
   a. Recall the emphasis on close contact with customers.
   b. This may be important not just to garner additional sales, but to predispose those of our customers who are early adopters to share their ideas for new products with us rather than with one of our rivals.

VIII. Product life cycles.
   A. The basic idea is that products have natural cycles.
     1. A birth period (in which products are first introduced).
     2. A growth period (in which their market size grows).
     3. A maturity period (in which growth slows).
     4. A decay period (in which the product loses market appeal and sales).[22]
   B. Table 4-3 provides the general features of the product life cycle.
   C. How long is each stage?
     1. Tremendous variation by industry.
       a. Some products seemingly never enter the decay phase (basic Coca-Cola and PepsiCo beverages have been mature for decades).
       b. Many people believe that, in general, product life cycles are shorter today than in the past.

        (2) **Defensive pricing** is the process of dropping price in response to a competitor's price drop.

           (a) This frequently occurs in the airline industry. When one player on a route drops price, typically so do other carriers on that route.[9]

           (b) You also sometimes see this with cars.

        (3) **Prestige (or premium) pricing** is the process of pricing at the top end of the range to convey, or maintain, a luxury or "high-end" image.

        (4) **Normal (or popular) pricing** is the process of pricing "in the middle."

3. **Cost-based pricing**.
   a. Pricing based on the cost of producing the product.
   b. **Mark-up pricing**: Add a fixed percent to the cost of the product (rather common in smaller retail shops and many restaurants).
   c. **Cost-plus pricing**: Price for a project is determined by adding a negotiated profit or fee to the actual costs incurred by the producer.
   d. **Break-even analysis**: A system that determines the relationship between the total costs of producing a product, the volume that must be sold to just "break even," and the profit (or loss) for volume above (or below) the "break even" quantity. I discuss this in detail below.

4. **Auction pricing**.
   a. Many auction pricing schemes exist, and the most common to many of you is the system used by eBay for auction items (not the "retailed priced" items which use one of the strategies discussed above).
   b. Conditional purchase pricing, also known as a reverse auction, has gained notoriety via its use by Priceline.com. Although variants were in use for many years, Priceline.com received a patent (on August 11, 1998) for the method and the "apparatus" to deliver the method to consumers. From the New York Times,[10] "Priceline . . . convinced the Patent and Trademark Office that it had invented a new way of doing business. . . ."
   c. For those not familiar with it, the original system works as follows:
       (1) Customers submit a credit card guaranteed bid via the web ("your own price") for, say, airline tickets with some set of conditions (say, dates of departure and flight on a major scheduled carrier).
       (2) Priceline.com then relays the bid to a number of airlines (unknown to the customer at this point) with whom they work.
       (3) The first airline accepting the bid gets it. (Certainly, it may be the case that no airline accepts the bid.)
       (4) While Priceline.com still uses this approach for airline tickets, they use other pricing strategies for other products.
   d. In auction pricing, the buyer sets the price for the product and the seller determines whether they are willing to sell for that price.

5. **Negotiated price**.
   a. The price of many products is negotiated.
   b. This is particularly true of complex industrial products, but we clearly see it in some retail goods such as automobiles.
   c. Indeed, in some societies "haggling" is a common practice even for many consumer goods.

6. General observations.
   a. Some firms choose and stick with a basic pricing strategy (for example, many small, independent retail shops use mark-up pricing more or less consistently).
   b. Firms often combine several pricing strategies for the same product (for example, the cell phone players seem to use a combination of demand and defensive pricing).
   c. Firms often target different market segments with different strategies. For example, the same national restaurant chain will often price differently for airport locations than for comparable in-town locations. As noted earlier this is an example of price discrimination.

      d. Firms often use one strategy for one class of products and a different strategy for a different class of product.

      e. Many other variations also exist.

C. Adjustments to basic pricing strategy.

   1. <u>Basic idea</u>: Assume a firm has a basic pricing strategy. "Adjustments" to this strategy are regular modifications that the firm will use under specific conditions or for specific types of products. Three common adjustments are . . .

      a. new product pricing,

      b. price reductions, and

      c. life cycle pricing.

   2. New product pricing.

      a. One standard situation is how the firm prices new products.

      b. Two adjustments can be identified:

        (1) **Price skimming**: Setting the highest possible price for a product during the introduction stage of its life cycle (example: Toshiba with their new laptops and HP for new hand-held calculators).

        (2) **Penetration pricing**: Setting low prices during product introduction in an attempt to build market share and perhaps inhibit the entry of other possible sellers (example: commonly used by Japanese auto producers during the early years of U.S. activity).

        (3) We've already discussed price as an entrance strategy for fast second movers, especially if the first mover pursues a price skimming strategy.

   3. Price reductions.

      a. **Price discrimination or "discounting"** is the process of charging different prices to different classes of customers.

        (1) Example: <u>The Wall Street Journal</u> has special student subscription rates.

        (2) Example: Many universities discount tuition for in-state students.

        (3) Please note: Discounting, as used here, is different from how the phrase "discount pricing" a few pages back.

      b. **Sales**: The act of offering for purchase a product or group of products at a reduced price for a limited period of time.

        (1) Some sales, such as back-to-school sales, are periodic devices to spur customer purchases.

        (2) Other sales are primarily to reduce inventory of a product, especially at the end of a sales season.

        (3) During the past year, we have seen many sales used to spur demand in a recessionary economic climate.

   4. Life cycle pricing is a planned adjustment to price as the product moves through its life cycle.

      a. A good example here is pricing for new cars. Usually price is low at the start of a model year, then increases, and then toward to end of the model year, they are again low.

      b. Please note: The **list price** remains constant throughout the entire model year (that large sticker on the car window)—what varies is the actual price charged. This is true for cars, but not for all products with life cycle pricing.

VII. What is the best approach to pricing?

A. No one objective is best for all firms in all circumstances.

   1. With the exception of survival pricing objectives, any of the remaining pricing objectives can be observed in successful firms.

   2. And given a specific objective, usually several different pricing strategies (or combinations) are viable.

B. Each pricing strategy has advantages and disadvantages. These are summarized Table 5-1 (below).

   1. For example, a competition-based strategy may be relatively insensitive to demand.

   2. As a second example, the conditional purchase strategy may work well for certain products and/or market segments, but may be too complicated for other products and/or segments.

Table 5-1   Advantages and Disadvantages of Various Approaches to Pricing

Approach	Advantages	Disadvantages
Demand based	Price adjusts to change in demand	Cost considerations may be overlooked
Competition based	Provides a core basis for differentiating the firm from other sellers	Difficult to adjust, especially in the short run
Cost based	Costs usually well incorporated into prices	May be insensitive to actual demand
Auction systems, including conditional purchase	Allows customers to set prices	May be inappropriate or too complicated for many goods or customers
Negotiated price	Particularly useful for complex industrial products where parties can often trade-off price and specifications	Can be time consuming and usually requires parties have a reasonable level of sophistication

C. Pricing in practice.
 1. First observation: Pricing decisions can be very straightforward or very complex in practice.
 2. Second observation: While it is critical to understand the basics, in practice we often see complex variations and combinations of the basics. Add in various forms of adjustment, and things can get very complicated.
 3. An excellent example here concerns the pricing of university education (remember my teaser at the beginning?), and a specific case we'll consider in class is the pricing of undergraduate education at Harvard and others.
 4. Important note: Most students tend to think that the seller always sets the price. Above we have seen situations in which the seller or the buyer set price or, as in negotiation when it could vary.

VIII. Break-even analysis.
 A. Important caveat.
  1. Most of you have some experience with break-even analysis, typically in economics, business calculus, managerial accounting, and/or high school.
  2. Our treatment here is conceptually identical to what you may have seen in other courses, but differs in two important ways:
   a. We are concerned with more typical applied problems.
   b. We are concerned with how firms may really use this type of analysis.
 B. Basics.
  1. First, we'll consider some vocabulary and some algebra. After the algebra, I provide a geometric approach, which most students find easier. Finally, you have a problem to try. The solution is provided.
  2. Vocabulary.
   a. **Total revenue**: The total sales of a product during a particular time period (also called total sales or just "sales") [Computed as . . .
     Total revenue = P (selling price per unit) $\times$ **Q** (quantity sold)].
   b. **Fixed costs**: Costs incurred no matter how many units of a product are produced or sold in a particular time period (examples: supervisory salaries; real estate taxes; insurance; mortgage, rent, or lease; etc).
     [**Fixed costs = F**]
   c. **Total variable costs**: Costs that depend (linearly) on the number of units produced in a particular time period (examples: direct materials; direct labor) [Computed as . . .
     Total variable costs = V (variable cost per unit) $\times$ **Q** (quantity sold)].

In this course we assume there are only two kinds of variable costs:[11]

(1) **Direct materials**: For our purposes, direct materials are the raw materials that can be physically and reasonably linked to the completed product (examples: the ink that becomes part of your newspaper; the chips that go into your PC).

(2) **Direct labor**: The labor that can be physically and reasonably linked to the actual production of the newspaper (example: the wages paid to the folks who run the presses that print your newspaper).

d. **Contribution margin (CM)**: Price per unit minus variable costs per unit, or **CM = P − V**
You can think of contribution margin as the money derived from each sale that "contributes" to covering the fixed cost of the project.

e. **Net Income (NI)**: An accounting measure of profit, computed as total revenue for a period minus total costs for the period:
NI = Total revenues − Total costs
NI = Sales − Total Variable Costs − Fixed Costs
NI = PQ − VQ − F
Since contribution margin = **P − V**, we can rewrite the above as
NI = (P − V)Q − F
NI = (CM)Q − F

C. **Break-even quantity and break-even price**:

1. **Break-even quantity**: The number of units that must be sold in the period for the total revenue (from all units sold) to equal exactly the total cost (of all units produced) for the period.

OK, we know   **(P − V)Q − F = NI**
at break-even   **(P − V)Q − F = NI = 0**
or   **(P − V)Q = F**
or break-even quantity: **Q★ = F/(P−V)**

2. **Break-even Price**: A similar bit of algebra can be used to solve for break-even price, which is
P★ = (F + VQ)/Q

D. **Geometric approach**: Putting all this together, we have Figure 5-2:

1. The x-axis measures quantity and the y-axis measures $$$.

2. Walking through Figure 5–2.

a. Fixed cost is independent of quantity and shown as a constant at all levels of quantity (for a given period).

b. Total variable cost is V × Q, and hence increases linearly with Q.

c. Total cost is variable plus fixed cost, shown as the sum of these two.

d. Revenue is P × Q, and hence increases linearly with Q.

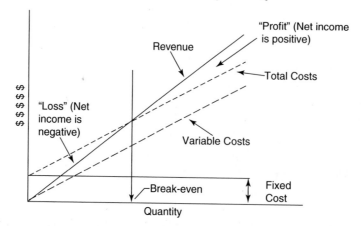

Figure 5-2   Break-even Analysis

e. The point at which the revenue and total cost curves intersect is the breakeven point.
   (1) The projection of this point onto the x-axis is the breakeven quantity.
   (2) At lower quantities, the total cost curve exceeds the total revenue curve, and hence the firm has a loss.
   (3) At higher levels, the total revenue curve exceeds the total cost curve, and hence the firm has a profit.

E. Remember our earlier discussion of the profit effects of dropping price?
   1. Now we can return to that discussion with some useful tools.
   2. First, let's use an algebraic approach. We know that the <u>break-even quantity is</u> $Q\star = F/(P-V)$
   3. Notice, as price is lowered (P gets smaller), (P − V) also gets smaller, which means that Q gets larger (i.e., break-even quantity gets larger).
   4. Is there some point at which no break-even is possible? Sure. When P = V, (P − V) = 0, and Q does not exist. Another way of saying this is: a necessary condition for break-even is that CM > 0.
   5. Finally, even if the contribution margin is positive, there is no guarantee that break-even will occur.
      a. Why?
      b. Several possibilities:
         (1) The break-even quantity may exceed the total demand in the market.
         (2) The break-even demand is less than total market demand, but represents a much larger market share than may be feasible for the firm to attain.
         (3) We may have capacity constraints—that is, the quantity required to break-even quantity exceeds our capacity to produce.
         (4) The market will not support the price required to achieve break-even.

F. Assumptions of the break-even model.
   1. There are a several assumptions that underlie break-even analysis.
   2. For our purposes, the important assumptions are as follows:
      a. Costs are either fixed or variable.
      b. Variable costs and revenues are linear over a wide range of quantity.
      c. Costs and prices will not change during the time period considered.
      d. The value of the dollar is constant over the time period considered.
      e. Worker productivity and machine productivity are constant over the time period considered.

IX. OK, now it's time to actually look at a break-even problem.

   A. Remember, I said at the start of this chapter that most of you have already seen break-even problems before, perhaps in micro-economics, in business calculus, or even in high school.
      1. In those courses, the problems are presented quite differently than what you'll see below.
      2. One difference is that the problem you'll see requires a certain amount of "bookkeeping" before you can solve it for breakeven price or quantity.
      3. A second difference is what I'll call the "criterion."
         a. Exactly what this means will become clear in a few minutes, but for the time being, let's think of it this way:
         b. In practice, breakeven analysis is often an <u>iterative process</u>.
            (1) That is, you collect a set of data regarding, say, fixed and variable costs and then solve, perhaps for breakeven price.
            (2) You might then look at that price and decide it is more than your customers will pay, perhaps because of serious price competition.
            (3) You then go back and try to see if there is some way you can reduce certain cost elements, and then "rerun" the analysis based on these adjusted costs elements.
            (4) In practice, this may need to be done several times.

   B. Hopefully, this will become more meaningful after you go through the example problem that follows at the end of this chapter.

Endnotes

1. Alfred Chandler, *The Visible Hand: the Managerial Revolution in American Business*, Cambridge, MA: Harvard University Press, 1977, p. 267. Apparently, this quote was one of Andrew Carnegie's favorite sayings.

2. The small number of sellers in oligopoly facilitates this. While theoretically possible in perfect competition, the huge number of players makes it effectively impossible.

3. The obvious form of price fixing involves sellers agreeing to all sell at more or less the same price. A more subtle approach is for sellers to agree that each will sell only in a particular geographical area, essentially allowing each to become a "local" monopolist. Curiously, it may also be illegal under U.S. case law for sellers to collude to lower prices [*Arizona v. Maricopa County Medical Society* (457 U.S. 332, 1982)]. The body of anti-trust law is massive, complex, and important.

4. "Samsung enters $90M settlement with states in price fixing case," *Pittsburgh Business Times*, February 6, 2007, accessed on February 11, 2007 at pittsburgh.bizjournals.com/pittsburgh/stories/2007/02/05/daily15.html?surround=lfn.

5. A. Lagorce, "British Airways fined in price-fixing settlement—Virgin not required to pay a penalty; no criminal proceedings yet," *MarketWatch*, http://www.marketwatch.com/news/story/british-airways-fined-650-million/story.aspx?guid=%7B288AE3F1%2DE4C6%2D4ECC%2D903A%2D785AF0296D8E%7D accessed December 3, 2007. The lead sentence is "British Airways Plc, Europe's third-largest airline, on Wednesday said it will pay fines of about $650 million to settle price-fixing probes with U.K. and U.S. regulators."

6. We develop the legal issues in a later set of notes.

7. Quote by Rodney Eckerman, music CEO of Clear Channel, the firm that then produced about 80 to 85 percent of the U.S. concert market, as reported by Jim Beckerman, of *The Record* (Bergen County, NJ) in "Concert audiences dwindle amid 'sticker shock,'" *Pittsburgh Post-Gazette*, August 26, 2001, pp. A, E5.

8. Ann Zimmerman, "*Très Cheap*: Taking aim at Costco, Sam's Club marshals diamonds and pearls," the *Wall Street Journal*, August 9, 2001, pp. A1, A4. This interesting article provides lots of information about competition among the two discount giants.

9. Recall our earlier discussion of collusive pricing. In footnote 3, above, collusion even for the purpose of dropping price is probably illegal [see *Arizona v. Maricopa County Medical Society* 457 U.S. 332 (1982)]. Defensive pricing is usually legal because the firm decreases price based on public information.

10. Peter H. Lewis, "A web concern gets patent for its model of business," the *New York Times*, August 10, 1998, pp. C1, C5.

11. If you have had some exposure to Managerial Accounting, you know there is a third element, namely, overhead. In practice, this is important, but for the purposes of this class, we consider overhead = 0.

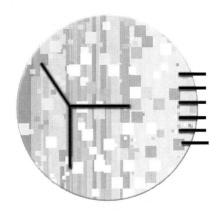

Active Practice

Active Practice for Chapter 5: How Much Should We Charge for Our Blue Tomatoes?

I. Example—Please tear out, solve, and bring to class

    A. Atkin Protection Services (APS) is in the business of supplying security cops to industrial customers. Regardless of how many security cops are assigned on any given day, APS must always have one sergeant on an 8-hour shift at a total cost of $200/shift. APS rents its office space at $1000/month and its computing system at $175/month. APS must also carry a fidelity bond, which is $2,400/year, as insurance against theft on the part of a guard. Each building covered requires one guard per shift, 21 shifts per week, at a cost of $125 per guard. Currently, APS has the opportunity to bid a job that involves providing guards for 25 buildings. Assume that APS would like to make an average net profit per month of $2000. How much should APS charge per building per shift? **How much should APS bid if the period covered by the bid is a month?**

    B. The solution is on the next page. BUT, before you flip to it, please try to solve it in the space below. Everything you need is on the proceeding few pages. Really.

II. **Solution**

   A. **Problem set-up**: The way to start is to go to the basic formula and solve it algebraically for what we want to find.

     1. Net income = Total sales revenue − Variable costs − Fixed costs

     2. $NI = PQ − VQ − F$

     3. What are we trying to find? Price. Hence, solving for P, we have . . .

       a. $PQ = NI + VQ + F$

       b. $P = (NI + VQ + F)/Q$

     4. OK, in order to solve for P, we need to find NI, V, Q, and F on a monthly basis (below I assume that 1 month = 30 days; if you assume 31 days, you get somewhat different results).

   B. **Fixed costs (F)**: Let's recall what we mean by fixed costs. They are costs incurred during the period independent of the quantity produced. What do we mean here by "quantity produced"? In this example, quantity produced refers to the number of building shifts for which we provide security services (if we provide service for one building on three shifts, we have 3 building shifts). OK, so what are these costs?

     1. Sergeant: Go back and reread the example. Note that it says "Regardless of how many security cops are assigned on any given day, APS must always have one sergeant on an 8-hour shift . . ." Hence, ($200/shift) × (3 shift/day) × (30 day/month) = **$18,000/month**

     2. Rent: We pay this regardless of how many buildings we service. Hence, = **$1,000/month**

     3. Bond: Again, we pay this regardless of how many buildings we service. Hence, ($2,400/year) × (1 year/12 month) = **$200/month**

     4. Computing system: Again, we pay this regardless of how many buildings we service. Hence, = **$175/month**

     5. **Total Fixed costs = $19,375/month**

   C. **Net Income desired (NI) = $2,000/month**

   D. **Variable costs (V)**: Let's make sure we remember what "variable costs" means. Variable costs are the costs incurred during the period that are dependent on the quantity produced. Specifically, we know these are typically direct material and direct labor. The example contains no information regarding direct material, and hence we will assume there is none. Is there any direct labor? Yes. For each building on each shift, we need a guard. Hence, (1 guard/building shift) × ($125/guard) = **$125/building-shift** From the information given, this is the only variable cost we incur.

   E. **Quantity**: Remember, we have already decided that quantity in this example refers to building-shifts for which provide security. (I know this sounds like a weird "quantity," but that's what it is.) OK, so how many building shifts are we bidding on? Let's see: 3 shifts a day, 30 days in a month, and 25 buildings . . . hence, (3 shift/day) × (30 day/month) × (25 buildings) = **2,250 building-shift/month**

   F. OK, putting all this together, we have . . .

      a. $P = (NI + VQ + F)/Q$

      b.   = {($2,000/month)
        + {($125/building shift) × (2,250 building-shift/month)}
        + $19,375/month}/(2,250 building shift/month)
        = $134.50/building shift

      c. or, per month
        = ($134.5/building shift) × (2,250 building shift/month)
        = **$302,625/month**

   G. Notice that the contribution margin is

     CM = $134.5/building shift − $125/building shift
       = $9.50/building shift per month

In other words, for each building-shift we provide security, APS makes $9.50 that goes toward covering fixed costs.

H. Ok, so far, so good.

1. So, now it's time to go visit the client. Suppose we put these numbers together in a nice presentation with lots of other information about client satisfaction and about how our price and quality looks great compared to other suppliers. We make our pitch with gusto.

2. After hearing us, assume they respond: "Thanks for your bid. We believe you are a competent and quality vendor. However, we are unwilling to pay more than $300,000 per month. Please review your numbers and see if you can get your bid down to $300,000/month. If you can, you've got a deal."

3. So, it's back in your court. **What do you do now?**

4. Were we in microeconomics, we would conclude that given these data, we have to get <u>at</u> <u>least</u> $302,625/month to accept the project. If the customer were unwilling to pay that price, APS shouldn't take the project.

5. However, as noted above, in practical business situations, we often view break-even problems as iterative. Now is the time to revisit your cost data and see if it can be reduced. Please do this and jot down your ideas on the next page.

This rest of page is left blank on purpose. Use it to jot down your ideas about "What to do now?" from the previous page.

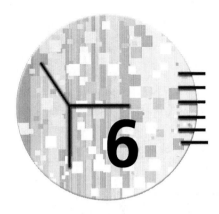

Linking Producers and Customers: Issues of Promotion and Channel Mix

6

> *"Where's the beef?"* [1]
>
> **Line from an old Wendy's commercial**

I. Teaser.
   A. The previous two chapters developed the basics of products, segments, and price. Now we turn to establishing the link between the product and the customer.
   B. You're a freshman and its time for a new laptop. How do you figure what is available and what is best for you? When asked, students last year said:
      1. "Huh?"
      2. "Ask around."
      3. "Check the web."
      4. "Whatever is obviously cheapest."
   C. More generally, how do you actually learn about products, manufacturers, and vendors? And how does the stuff actually get from producer to retailer to you?
      1. To the first question, many of you may say word-of-mouth or advertising or TV commercials or banner ads. All of these all important, of course, but is that it?
      2. To the second, most probably say, "I don't know . . . trucks?" Again, a small part of the answer.
   D. Effective and efficient promotion and distribution are the hallmarks of a productive modern economy. Promotion you know about, as each of us has something to say about how we learn about products, producers, and retailers. Distribution, on the other hand, is less obvious. We now turn to a discussion of both.

II. Review of marketing concepts to this point.
   A. So far, we have developed the following ideas:
      1. Sellers in perfect competition generally have little or no control over prices and little or no opportunities for profit
      2. Hence, sellers have significant incentives to be innovative to gain some level of control over pricing and profits.
      3. This produces four possible strategies, each with economic costs, potential benefits, and significant risk. Please see Table 6–1.
      4. To this point, we've detailed only "stay" and product differentiation, although the other two were outlined in Chapter 2.

Table 6–1   Strategies Available to Producers in Perfect Competition

Strategy	Cost	Benefit	Risk
Stay in perfect competition	No incremental cost	No incremental benefit	No incremental competitive advantage over rivals; no L-T profit
Enhance product (Product differentiation)	Incremental costs required to invest in product differentiation	Opportunity to develop new product, gain customers, and increase profit	Not turning the investment into sufficient product development, resulting in • loss of the investment • no gain in advantage over rivals • threat to the firm's survival
Enhance process (Improve productivity)	Incremental costs required to invest in process/productivity enhancement	Opportunity to reduce costs and prices, gain customers, and increase profit	Not turning the investment into sufficient process enhancement, resulting in • loss of the investment • no gain in advantage over rivals • threat to the firm's survival
Change business model	Incremental costs required to invest in the new business model	Opportunity to find new ways to "make money"	Not turning the investment into a successful new business model, resulting in • loss of the investment • no gain in advantage over rivals • threat to the firm's survival

B. Product differentiation.
   1. Product differentiation can be achieved in several ways:
       a. Development of a novel product.
       b. Modification of an existing product, which can be accomplished via . . .
           (1) product extension or
           (2) product refinement.[2]
   2. Firms may choose to differentiate products via being a first mover or a second mover, and if a second mover, as a fast or slow mover. Each choice has advantages and disadvantages.
   3. Many, perhaps most, new products fail. Differentiation tends to be more successful when there exists a customer segment which prefers the differentiated product to the existing generic (or other differentiated) product.
       a. Buyer preference (or utility) can be subdivided into form, place, time, and transaction utilities.
       b. Although each buyer has unique preferences for any given product, we also assume that many buyers have similar utility functions. Segments are sets of buyers with similar utility functions.
           (1) Utility functions are not directly visible or easily measured directly. Therefore, we use more visible surrogates to identify segments.
           (2) These segmentation variables include various demographic, economic, geographical, and social/psychological factors.
       c. Competition based on modification of the product's ability to deliver incremental aspects of any (or all) of these utilities is called non-price competition.
   4. Buyers may shop on price, value, or status. In practice, buyers usually do not know all sellers, but shop from a constrained set.
   5. Branding is an important aspect of product identification and value enhancement. The total value of the brand to the producer or retailer is brand equity.
   6. Products have life cycles and at various points in the product life cycle, there are different opportunities to differentiate further or to reduce costs.
   7. Pricing is a decision-making process that may be the purview of the seller or the buyer, which assumes there may be multiple possible objectives that each party is trying to achieve and multiple possible strategies.

C. Before we leave our discussion of product differentiation, two more topics still need to be developed. These two, the focus of these notes, are . . .
   1. the **promotion mix** (or **marketing communication mix**) and
   2. the **channel mix** (or **distribution channels**).

III. Promotion mix.
   A. What is promotion mix?
      1. Recall our earlier "alternative" definition of marketing was *"the process by which one party in a market attempts to increase the likelihood that they strike the transactions that they wish to strike."* Elements of this process that we have discussed so far include
         a. pricing and price,
         b. product differentiation and customer segmentation, and
         c. branding.
      2. Another element is promotion mix.
      3. In general terms, promotion mix is the communication linkage between the parties in the transaction. As typically used, the phrase "promotion mix" refers to **the set of methods used to manage the customer buying process over time**.[3]
         a. Central to this process is a delicate balance between influencing the customer to purchase, satisfying the needs of the customer, and retaining the customer over time.
         b. This balance is an important and subtle adjustment to Chapter 4.
         c. Let's think about this balance for a second with a specific example.
            (1) There are thousands of colleges and universities in the U.S., and all need students.
            (2) Most of them attempt "to increase the likelihood of striking the transactions they wish to strike," which is a gentle way of saying most engage in aggressive marketing of those high school juniors and seniors they want as students (and, of course, also to their parents). This is the influence process.
            (3) The easiest way to influence the potential student is to tell them what they want to hear, even if not accurate. For example, say that university x makes gourmet food available when you visit campus leading you to believe that you'll get steak (or premium tofu) for dinner every evening. Certainly, you could check this out by asking lots of students, but generally you are not that aggressive.
            (4) If **all** I wanted to do was influence you to attend university x, I might tell you lots of stuff, much of it just not accurate. Just may work. So, you choose university x. How long does it take you until you discover "the truth"? A few days? A few weeks or months? Whatever— when you find out you won't be happy—and needs you thought would be filled, aren't.
            (5) Will university x retain you as a customer? Best answer is that many of you will be strongly predisposed to leave and many will.
         d. The point is, **many things that may cause you to "buy" aren't the same things that make you happy after you have bought**.
            (1) Finding a balance among influence, real satisfaction of need, and customer retention is a difficult task.
            (2) Managing this balance involves use of marketing communication before, during, and after the purchase decision.[4]
      4. Promotion mix, product mix, and customer segments.
         a. These three concepts are different, but interdependent.
         b. Different types of communications (promotion mix) may be better or worse in influencing different kinds of customers (segments) to be attracted to and to buy different kinds of products (product mix).
         c. In other words, the firm must carefully match promotion mix, product mix, and segmentation to achieve an effective and efficient increase in the likelihood that they strike the transactions that they wish to strike over the long run.

B. Elements in the promotion mix.
  1. The standard elements of the promotion mix include the following:
     a. **Advertising**: There are many forms of advertising and most of us have significant experience with them.
        (1) All involve a paid, usually impersonal[5] persuasive presentation of products, product concepts, or product-relevant parties by a sponsor.
        (2) Advertising can use any of a number of different **media**, ranging from TV to posters to traditional print ads.[6]
        (3) Additionally, advertising frequently makes use of celebrities to endorse products.[7]
     b. **Sales promotion**: Short-term incentives, such as coupons, contests, free samples, to induce purchase or trial use of a good or service. The difference between sales promotion and advertising is that the former provides a tangible incentive.
     c. **Personal selling**: Personal, face-to-face, persuasive interaction, including sales presentation, order taking, and customer assistance.
     d. **Direct marketing**: Various impersonal methods to communicate with and solicit orders from prospective customers, including catalogs, telemarketing, and the Internet.[8]
     e. **Public relations**: Various programs to build, maintain, or change the image of a firm, its brands, or its products, including sponsorships, annual reports and other publications, and press releases. As an example to you sports fans: Think about 3Com Park or PNC Park.
     f. **Miscellaneous**: Many other factors can reinforce (or detract) from the persuasive aspects of the traditional promotion mix elements, including product packaging, styling, and logos, store location, styling, and general appearance, and so on.
  2. Often a particular "item" can simultaneously serve more than one of the elements.
     a. For example, an unsolicited catalog received in the mail is primarily a direct marketing tool.
     b. However, it could also provide advertising, could provide a sales promotion, and helps project a public relations image.
C. **The overall objective is to produce an optimally effective promotion mix constrained by budget**.
  1. Therefore, the basic decision process concerns finding the particular set of these elements that will be most effective in managing the buying process across multiple products and multiple segments.
  2. Some observations.
     a. **There is no one best mix for all products and customer segments**.
     b. Even within an industry, there is often considerable divergence across rivals.
        (1) For example, in cosmetics Estée Lauder uses considerable print and TV advertisement, and retail promotions,
        (2) while Avon makes much use of personal selling.
     c. Different segments may require different promotion mix even for the same product.
        (1) For example, long-distance carriers tend to use one form of sales promotion for college students (usually freebies, such a T-shirts),
        (2) while different sales promotions (such as free minutes) often work better for older folks.
     d. Effective promotion mix may vary across product life cycle.
        (1) Kotler speculates that sales promotion may be more effective in a product's mature and decline phases than during its growth phase,
        (2) while advertising may be more effective during the introduction phase than in the decline phase.[9]
     e. Budget constraints are real.
        (1) For example, you may wish to advertise your product to sports-oriented males ages twenty-five to thirty-five.
        (2) One way may be a Super Bowl TV commercial, but that could easily cost you a million bucks more or less, and that may be way outside of your budget.
        (3) So you might opt instead to spend $150,000 on a combination of print ads in <u>Sports Illustrated</u> and commercials during NBA games.

  D. Final comment.
  1. Promotion mix
      a. is a decision-process
      b. selecting among many possible elements
      c. constrained by a budget
      d. to manage a critical link between seller and buyer
      e. where no one choice is ideal for all buyers, products, sellers, or situations.
  2. We have just touched the surface of this central function of marketing, and for some of you, this may be a career field.

IV. Channel mix basics.

  A. Some key terms.
  1. **Distribution** to refer to the general phenomenon of moving product from raw material through to manufactures and to end-users.
  2. A **distribution system** can refer either to the distribution process of a part of a firm, a single firm, an entire industry, or the economy as a whole.
  3. **Market channels** refer to intermediaries between a seller and either its immediate buyers or the ultimate end user.
  4. **Supply channels** are between the seller and its input vendors.
  5. **Channel mix** refers to the specific set of decisions a firm uses to manage its market channels (this phrase is sometimes used also to refer to managing supply channels, but here we assume it applies only to market channels).
  6. Other terms you'll come across are **supply chain** and **logistics**.
      a. For a long time, logistics referred to the formal study of distribution systems (there is a huge, rich set of mathematical modeling tools for example) and applications of the results of these studies.
      b. Today, both are frequently used as synonyms for distribution system. I'll use either "supply chain" or "distribution system."
  B. Two important concepts.
  1. The overall goal of effective supply chain management (SCM) is getting the right amount of the right product in the right place at the right time. The lower the cost of accomplishing this, the more efficient.
      a. Although parts of the supply chain can be vertically integrated, we start with the most basic idea—namely, all players in the supply chain are independent firms.
      b. If so, then the type of transaction that "holds the chain together" is a market transaction. Hence, the achievement of this goal cannot be coordinated by a single firm. Rather, it has to be advantageous to all firms in the chain to achieve this coordination.
      c. To understand one such advantage, we need to examine the concept of estimated demand.
  2. Estimated demand: Assume for a minute we consider a retailer. Before the retailer can put stock in the shelves, it must order product. And before it can order product, it must decide how much of what stock keeping unit (SKU) to order. This is the estimated demand issue—i.e., the retailer will order so as to fill its estimation of buyer demand.
      a. Methods of estimation.
          (1) Demand may be estimated by informal methods ("I think we'll sell about a thousand of this item").
          (2) Demand may be estimated by formal statistical methods (usually regression or econometric techniques).
      b. Estimated demand. . .
          (1) may be exactly correct, and hence, after actual demand is observed, supply exactly equals demand;
          (2) may be too high, resulting in excess inventory (leading to excess costs—why?);
          (3) may be too little, resulting in stockouts (resulting in lost revenues and unhappy buyers).

    c. Please recall the goal of effective SCM—the right amount of the right stuff in the right place at the right time.

        (1) This implies getting the estimation of demand as close to the future actual demand as is possible.

        (2) And this suggests why all parties may find this goal as advantageous, namely, no player will incur the added costs of excess inventory and no player will lose revenue or customers due to stockouts.

V. Linking manufacturers and end users.

  A. Clearly, some manufacturers sell directly to end users.

    1. An **end user** is the ultimate customer—the agent in the market who actually uses the product. For simplicity, we will use "manufacturer" to refer to the firm that produces this product. Inputs to manufacturers are often also "manufactured," but we will use the term "intermediate goods" producer to distinguish them.

    2. Dell is an example of a manufacturer that pioneered selling PCs directly to the end user. Visit Dell's website and they will sell you a computer that they make.

    3. Yet, many producers, probably most producers, do not sell directly to the end users of the product.

      a. For example, you buy a Ford Explorer not directly from Ford, but from an independent dealer. Typically, you don't buy clothes directly from Polo Ralph Lauren but from some retail shop.

      b. This is also true for services. For example, most of us "buy" our credit cards not directly from Visa or MasterCard, but from banks that buy the service from Visa or MasterCard and resell it to us.

  B. Why don't all manufacturers sell directly to end users?

    1. There are many reasons.

      a. **Cost**: The sheer cost of selling directly to all possible customers may be prohibitive.

        (1) For example, there are potentially 300 million, or so, potential purchasers of Levi's jeans in the U.S. The sheer cost of setting up and running shops to provide a convenient point of sale to all of these potential customers may be overwhelming.

        (2) Please note how the evolution of e-commerce may change this.

      b. **Feasibility**: Variation on the cost theme—the sheer feasibility of establishing and running all those shops is questionable.

      c. **Relative profitability**: The profitability of running just a manufacturing operation may be greater than running both a manufacturing and direct-selling-to-the-end-user operation.

      d. **Product complementarity**: It may be that sales of one firm's product increase if another firm's products are available at the same site. Those jeans, for example, may be hotter sellers if they are available in the same shops that carry other firms' shirts or sweaters.

      e. **Value-added services**: An intermediary may provide services that enhance the sale of the product. For example, an independent car dealer may carry cars produced by several different manufacturers, thereby allowing you to make a purchase decision without having to run to a million different locations. They also service your car.

      f. **Relative organizational skills**: Most firms have specialized skills. Some, for example, may just not "have the skills" to sell effectively to the end user and may see investment in continued development of existing manufacturing skills as producing better long-term returns.

    2. I don't have specific data, but I suspect that most manufacturers do not sell directly to end-users for some combination of the above listed reasons.

  C. What flows through a marketing channel?

    1. The obvious answer is the physical product. This is true, but other important "things" also flow through marketing channels, including. . .

      a. title, or formal documents pertaining to ownership,

      b. information, which may concern the product, a customer, the producer, or a channel element,

      c. promotion, which we've just talked about, and/or

      d. payment.

2. Which produces different types of marketing channels as developed in Chapter 4.
   a. For example, some medicine you needed last month may have moved from manufacturer to wholesaler to retailer to you, aided by various physical transporters in between.
   b. Payment, however, probably moved electronically through several banks (between the manufacturer and the wholesaler, between the wholesaler and the retailer, between you and the retailer), using no physical transporters.
D. Channel design.
   1. Firms must decide what marketing channels they will use to distribute their products.
   2. The specifics evolve as a result of what rivals do (or don't do) and the relative costs, opportunities, and availability of channels.
      a. For example, in the early days of PCs, IBM had a large, existing sales force well experienced in selling computers to industry.
         (1) "Surprise" #1. They used the same sales force to sell their early PCs.
         (2) "Surprise" #2. They sold these PCs directly to firms as end-users, not households or individuals.
         (3) Selling directly to end users, whether the end user is a firm or a person, is called a **direct-marketing** (or zero-level) channel. ("Zero level" refers to zero intermediaries.)
         (4) Notice that IBM used IBM sales people to construct its direct channel; today, Dell uses a website with no sales people as a direct channel.
      b. Compaq, which began selling IBM clones soon after IBM entered the business was a new firm, had no sales force, and had little money to start a sales force.
         (1) From relatively early on, they sold their PCs to retail stores (such as Sears) who in turn sold them to the end user.
         (2) At the time, this significantly increased the availability of PCs to households.
         (3) However, it was not particularly useful in reaching firms as end users (similarly, IBM's sale force had little or no impact on households).
         (4) Such an approach, involving one intermediary (usually a retailer although sometimes a wholesaler) is a **one-level channel**.
      c. In other instances, we observe a **two-level channel** in which the manufacturer sells to a wholesaler who sells to a retailer who sells to the end user. As an example, most pharmaceuticals are sold this way.
      d. More complex patterns sometimes occur.
   3. The end user's needs may influence channel choice.
      a. Direct channels work well when the customer has need for a single product or for a class of products all manufactured by the producer.
         (1) This works reasonably well, for example, for PCs, but not for office products.
         (2) The customer may wish to buy pads of paper, pencils, paper clips, and copy machine toner from a single source, yet it is unlikely that one firm makes all these products.
      b. Direct channels work well when the product needs no installation, or when the end user has installation expertise. Just the opposite is true when installation is something the end user cannot, or will not do.
         (1) For example, most PCs are either ready-to-use or installation issues can be covered by an 800 number.
         (2) However, most homeowners (end users) don't have the expertise to re-shingle the roof of their homes.
      c. This can get very complicated, but the main theme is that knowledge of the end user's needs is important in the design of channels.
   4. Availability and appropriateness of channels.
      a. All channels have a limited capacity, just as manufacturing facilities do.
         (1) For example, a retailer may have only a limited amount of shelf space it can devote to a particular class of products.
         (2) When a particular channel is satiated, alternatives need to be found or developed.

(3) For example, Avon developed its door-to-door personal selling system as a direct result of not being able to find adequate shelf space in department stores.

   b. Any particular channel has advantages and disadvantages.

     (1) For example, Walmart as a retail channel has the advantage of size and presence throughout the country.

     (2) However, for products that have a luxury image, Wall-Mart's low price policy may be inappropriate, since it may detract from the luxury image of the product.

5. Choice of channel is likely dependent on costs.

   a. Channels "make money" by selling the product for more than they paid for it.

     (1) Typically, this passes through to the end user. All things equal, when more intermediary channels are involved, the price to the end user tends to increase.

     (2) This can be a problem if the final cost is higher than the customer would have to pay for a substitute product that moved through fewer channels.

   b. Some channels are simply more efficient than others, in the sense of improving speed or accuracy, or not adding significantly to the price paid by the end user.

6. **Backward channels** are market channels which link the end user backward to the retailer, wholesaler, or manufacturer.

   a. Obvious examples include the recycling of glass and aluminum containers back to bottle or can manufacturers.

   b. Nucor, a steel maker, pioneered a type of steel production that requires scrap steel as a raw material.

   c. I consider the trade-in of an old model car as part of a new car purchase to be another example.

VI. The effects of instability or high costs of maintaining stability in the distribution system

  A. In the above discussion, we (tacitly) assumed that the various players in the distribution system, including the marketing channels, were independent businesses.

   1. This implies that the transactions between the players are market transactions.

   2. We know from earlier material that most market transactions are relatively stable most of the time in advanced economies (in the sense of relatively stable price, product attribute, and availability). Please recall that this stability is a result of normal market forces and regulatory mechanisms, the latter of which have real cost, except in the case of pure interpersonal trust. Also, if markets are stable, most transactions are likely to be spot (why?).

  B. Causes of instability.

   1. Instability can arise from normal fluctuation. For example, agricultural raw materials (think of corn, coffee, and cocoa beans) have normal fluctuation caused by growing seasons.

   2. Instability can arise from random effects. Many possible examples, but perhaps the easiest to think about are the effects of unusual weather conditions on agricultural products.

   3. Instability can arise from vendor action, such as quality out of normal specification or missed deliveries. These could be from normal or random causes.

   4. Instability can arise from the buyer side. Students usually have some difficulty understanding this one. As an example, let's assume you are a manufacturer and you sell to a retailer. If a retailer runs a sale on your products, it may cause stockout or require a larger than normal supply from you. Even if they put other products on sale, it may affect your product (by abnormally reducing demand for your stuff or by increasing demand because your stuff is a complementary product).

  C. What happens if these market transactions are not stable or if the transaction costs are great?

   1. We'll first consider the case if stability cannot be maintained. Then we will consider the case of high transaction costs.

   2. In both cases, we observe a disruptive effect on the distribution system. For example, if I am a manufacturer and there is instability between "me" and a supplier of raw material, I . . .

     a. can't be certain I'll have the amount of RM I need when I need it, or

     b. can't be certain it will have the attributes I need, or

    c. can't reasonably estimate the price of the RM, or

    d. some combination of these.

  3. Hence, I need to do something or my ability to deliver product to my customers is threatened.

  4. Similarly, assume I am a manufacturer selling through a one channel system to my end users. Could there be instability or high transaction costs between me and my retailer? Sure, although it may take slightly different form.

    a. For example, perhaps the retailer has relative power over me (of the type discussed in Chapter 3). If so, the retailer may constantly push me to reduce my price (to him) even though he continues to sell to the end user at the same retail price.

    b. Or, perhaps the retailer sells many different brands (think of retailer of PCs, think that you are Apple, and the retailer also sells Toshiba, Acer, and other brands of PC) and you believe (for whatever reason) that the retailer doesn't sell your product as aggressively as that of your rivals who use the same retailer.

    c. Both of these are forms of instability (first case is analogous to price instability regarding raw material and the second is analogous to the availability issue). We can also identify situations of high transaction costs.

  5. Hence, as before, my ability to deliver product to my end user customer is threatened.

D. Vertical marketing systems.

  1. What could my firm do?

    a. I could switch suppliers (or retailers).

    b. I could increase the use of future transactions.

    c. I could develop some kind of a special relationship with the supplier (or retailer).

    d. I could develop or acquire a supplier (or retailer), becoming, in essence my own supplier (or retailer).

  2. In practice, each of these four changes the nature of the existing market transaction. The latter two produce fundamental change in the distribution system called vertical marketing systems.

    a. Switching suppliers (or retailers) maintains a market transaction but with a different party.

    b. Increasing the use of future transactions also maintains a market transaction, but of a different type.

    c. Developing a special relationship maintains a market transaction but superimposes some (perhaps significant) constraints.

    d. Developing my own supplier (or retailer) changes the transaction from market to transfer. We refer to this as a **corporate** vertical market system or **vertical integration**.

E. OK, now let's first consider **corporate vertical market systems (or vertical integration)**, which appear in two forms.

  1. <u>One version occurs when one party in the distribution system becomes their own customer</u>, e.g., a manufacturer **forward integrates** to become its own wholesaler or retailer.

    a. For example, beer producers in Great Britain typically own pubs (not surprisingly, your choices are limited to the brands produced by the manufacturer).

    b. In Japan, auto manufacturers own retail showrooms.

    c. Another interesting example is Amerada-Hess. This firm began as an explorer of petroleum deposits and a driller. Over time, it forward integrated into shipping, refining, distribution of refined products, and finally, retail gasoline sales (under the brand name Hess, which should be familiar to those of you from New Jersey and the Philadelphia area).

    d. A highly visible recent example is Apple (the manufacturer) developing and opening Apple Stores (the retailer).

  2. <u>Another version occurs when one party in the distribution system becomes their own supplier.</u> For example a manufacturer **backward integrates** to become its own component or raw material supplier.

    a. For example, years ago GM developed Delphi (and Ford, Visteon) as suppliers of many of the components used in the manufacture of their vehicles.

    b. Ford is particularly interesting. It began as an auto maker, but by the 1930s had backward integrated to the mining of iron ore. Indeed, Mr. Ford, a strong believer in vertical integration, built something called the Rouge River complex, which (in theory at least) was to have iron ore come in one end of the plant and cars out the other side.

3. How does vertical integration reduce the instability problem?

    a. Presumably, by becoming your own supplier (or customer) you can reduce instability relative to the market situation exactly because you now can control the supplier (or customer) directly since they are now a part of your firm.

    b. Notice, the firm has "converted" what was a market transaction to a transfer transaction.

4. Could this also be used in the case where the market is stable, but the cost to maintain stability is great?

    a. Yes.

    b. Why? If the cost of developing the supplier (or retailer) AND managing it is lower than the cost to maintain market transaction stability, the firm reduces its costs.

    c. Special language is used here: the cost of maintaining market stability is called a **transaction cost**[10] and the cost of building and operating the new unit is called the **cost of hierarchy**.

5. This produces an important principle, namely, <u>the trigger for vertical integration is when the expected transaction costs exceed the expected hierarchy costs</u>.

F. The alternatives.

1. The simplest approach is to simply change vendors or customers if possible.

2. A second approach, not always available, is to shift from mostly spot to a greater concentration of future transactions.

3. A third approach for downstream issues is exclusive or limited distribution.

    a. <u>Exclusive distribution</u> occurs when the upstream player (usually a manufacturer) decides to distribute to the end user via only one retailer (although that retailer may have multiple shops).

    b. <u>Limited distribution</u> occurs when the upstream player (again, usually the manufacturer) decides to distribute to the end user via a small number of specially selected retailers (and again, each may have multiple shops). Limited distribution is quite common in upscale apparel and high-end jewelry and watches.

    c. In addition to resolving issues associated with stability or transaction costs, exclusive or limited distribution is often part, effectively, part of the promotion mix of both the retailer and the manufacturer, in the sense that limited distribution may build brand image (to both parties).

4. There are analogous methods for upstream issues.

    a. <u>Sole sourcing</u> is when the downstream player decides to use only one supplier of some product. Although the term is different, it is essentially a version of exclusive distribution upstream.

    b. A second possibility is called using a <u>captive supplier</u>. In this case, the downstream player attempts to control the supplier by becoming the suppliers only customer (or overwhelmingly largest customer).

5. Please note that in all four cases (exclusive or limited distribution, sole source or captive supplier), the focal firm attempts to establish some level of stability within the context of maintaining a market (as opposed to a transfer) relationship.

    a. The benefits and risks (in all four cases) to each party are complex.

    b. For example, a benefit that a captive supplier may enjoy is that they have less need to find new customers but at the serious risk of not enough (or no) customers if the dominant customer decides to slow (or stop) buying. The customer has the benefit of control over the supplier (by threat to leave) which can frequently produce lower prices from the supplier or specific types of differentiated product, but at the risk that if the supplier fails, it may have important implications. In the particular case of a captive supplier, usually the supplier has greater risk and less benefit than the customer.

6. More complicated, but very common, are franchise agreements.

    a. For example, many McDonald's stores are not owned by the McDonald's firm, but by **franchisees** that have a contractual relationship with McDonalds (called the **franchiser**).

        (1) This allows an independent business to sell McDonald's products with the obvious benefit of selling an established brand. The risks are again complex. For example, the franchiser may allow too many franchisees in a region, depleting potential demand to each. Also, problems at one franchisee may spill over to others (for example, the outbreak of E. coli bacteria at Taco Bells in one part of the country two years ago may have had serious effects on Taco Bell franchisees in other parts of the country).

        (2) Similarly, the benefits and risks to the franchiser are complex. Benefits range from wider product distribution without the cost of establishing shops to franchisees having better local market knowledge than may be possible for a large national (or international) franchiser. Risks include ineffective franchisees.

    b. A huge number of firms operate this way, from fast food to both low-end motel and high-end hotel chains to termite exterminators to insurance providers.

G. OK. Let's return to vertically integrated systems for some additional ideas.

    1. The basic concept of vertical integration has significant appeal.

        a. Let's take Mr. Ford's view for a second.

        b. If he could control the supply line "all the way back" to raw materials, he might have several big time advantages:

            (1) He could control the flow of raw and intermediate material and therefore not have to worry about world supply.

            (2) He could better control the price of raw and intermediate materials, and therefore not have as much worry about world price.

            (3) He could control the quality of raw and intermediate material and therefore not have to worry about quality.

            (4) He could, in essence take the profit that would have otherwise flowed to independent businesses.

            (5) If he were successful in controlling a significant amount of critical raw or intermediate goods, he might have a huge competitive advantage over other, non-integrated car makers.

            (6) Sounds great, eh?

        c. However, vertical integration often doesn't actually produce these results. Why?

            (1) If your firm owns its suppliers and it sole sources from these suppliers, than your firm is insulated from the normal competitive forces of the market. The same is true for forward integration.

            (2) Now remember our discussion in Chapter 2: It is competition from the market that provides firms with the incentive to learn how to make new products and/or to learn how to reduce costs.

            (3) If your vertically integrated supplier is captive, (i.e., sells only your firm), the supplier tends to lose the incentive to innovate product or develop lower costs methods of operation.

                (a) Why?

                (b) They don't have to compete against other suppliers.

                (c) They don't have to worry about convincing other buyers to buy "their stuff."

            (4) Similarly, if your vertically integrated customer sole sources from your firm (i.e., buys only from you) it loses contact with the benefit of innovation by other suppliers.

            (5) Economists refer to this by saying that markets tend to be more efficient than hierarchies (i.e., often the long run cost for innovative product is lower when bought from a competitive rather than a captive market).

            (6) This produces some interesting and not obvious conclusions.

(a) When environments are very complex, there are often incentives to vertically integrate. However, if the firm does vertically integrate, this may result in rapid, significant loss of market information, quickly dissipating initial benefits.

(b) And when environments are less complex, the incentive to vertically integrate may be trivial. However, the long term benefits may be great, exactly because market information is not changing rapidly.

(c) That is, when markets "fail" (i.e., they are not stable or it is very expensive to maintain stability) vertical integration may be superior in the short run. But if the market failure is associated with rapid change in the market, the vertical integration benefits may erode rapidly.[11]

2. <u>Bottom line</u>: Vertical integration has both positives and negatives.

   a. Sometimes vertical integration is powerful; sometimes it isn't.

   b. At a given time, it may be more powerful for certain firms in an industry and less powerful for other firms in the same industry.[12]

   c. The general trend today is for firms that historically were vertically integrated to sell (or "spin off") business other than their core business.

   (1) That is, the general trend today is away from vertical integration.

   (2) This produces many business relationships that may look strange.

       (a) For example, in the auto industry, many car makers buy supplies made by other car producers.

       (b) But we already talked about this (back in Chapter 2) when the concept of competitor was introduced (there I said, "This definition of competitors implies that a party who is your rival in one market may be your ally in another.")

3. One last link to previous material. In Chapter 3, we introduced the concept of focus and diversification. Vertically integrated firms are usually a form of related diversification.

H. Horizontal marketing systems.

1. Horizontal marketing systems emerge when entities (which could be multiple units of one firm or separate firms) at the same level in the distribution system join forces to enhance the sale of each other's products.

2. A good local example concerns Giant Eagle and some bank. In most new Giant Eagle stores, you will find a PNC or Citizen's Bank.

   a. Presumably, this arrangement provides advantages to both.

   (1) By providing the opportunity to do your banking while you do your food shopping may increase the likelihood that consumers will shop at Giant Eagle rather than an alternative.

   (2) Conversely, the convenience of banking at the same place you shop may cause some shoppers to switch to the bank over an alternative.

   b. While such systems provide certain advantages, there is no guarantee of success.

3. Another interesting example exists with Barnes & Noble and Starbucks.

4. Please note: While the discussion above implies that these firms are from unrelated industries, this is not necessary. For example, a food court is a form of a horizontal marketing system. An interesting horizontal system of units from the same firm in the same industry is what I call "KenTacoHut," a system involving setting up a KFC, a Taco Bell, and a Pizza Hut (all owned by Yum Brands) in its own food court.

VII. Comparing promotion and channel mix.

A. While these two are obviously quite different in detail, the two are really quite similar conceptually.

B. Conceptual similarities.

1. Both are complex decision processes.

2. The decision process requires choice among many possible elements (where elements of the promotion mix involve such things as the relative emphasis on personal selling and where elements of the channel mix include such things as working through retailers or directly with the end user).

   3. Both involve making choices under budget constraints.
   4. Both involve management of the critical link between producer and customer.
   5. And, in both cases, there is no one mix that is ideal for all customers, products, producers, or situations.
   C. Interaction between promotion mix, channel mix, and production system.
      1. Just as choice of promotion mix is dependent in part on access to specific customers in specific segments regarding specific products, so to does promotion mix depend in part on channels.
      2. Example: Assume a product distributed via a one-level channel. Question: Should the producer target its promotion mix at the **retailer** (attempting to influence the retailer to purchase our product), or should it target **the end users** (attempting to increase the likelihood that they will demand the product from the retailer?)
         a. Targeting the promotion mix to the retailer (or any intermediary) is a **push strategy**. Presumably, if we (as the producer) are successful in inducing the intermediary to buy the product, the intermediary will "push" the product through to the end user.
         b. Targeting the promotion mix to the end user is a **pull strategy**. Presumably, if successful, we should induce the end user to "pull" the product from the retailer.
      3. While the above is the standard definition of push and pull (when viewed solely as two forms of promotion strategy), I think the whole issue is more complex. This is due to how the same terms tend to be used in operations (as opposed to marketing).
         a. In operations, a pull system is one in which the downstream player (usually the end user) is the trigger for production, while a push system is one in which the upstream player estimates demand and produces product to meet this estimate.
         b. Putting these two together, then, looks not just the target of the promotion mix, but also at the trigger for the production of the product. If the target of the promotion mix is the end user AND the product is not produced until the end user acts, we have a "pure" pull system in my view.
         c. As an example, consider McDonald's and Burger King. Both are zero-channel and both target their promotion mix to the end user.
            (1) However, McDonald's estimates the number of burgers likely to be demanded in some time period and produces to that estimate. Result, a standard product is there waiting for your order.
            (2) On the other hand, at BK your order is the trigger for the burger to be assembled.
            (3) That is, at McD's the trigger for the order is the estimate of demand (what, how much, and when), while at BK, the customer order is the trigger.
         d. A pure "push" system would not target the end user and end user action would not trigger production. As an example, think of something like Domino sugar (or Morton salt). While we see occasional sales promotion to the end user in the form of coupons, I haven't observed a real effort to target the end user. Also, the manufacturers produce to demand estimates.
      4. The general trend today in marketing is toward pull strategies. A similar trend exists also in operations, although it seems more modest. While "pure pull" (both marketing AND operations) may be easier to accomplish in zero-level channel mixes, we do see pure pull systems in complex multi-channel mixes in some commercial settings. For example, Toyota manufactures cars via a complex, pure pull system that extends backward not just to direct suppliers but to their suppliers (and sometimes even further back).

VIII. OK, we have now completed our discussion of marketing issues.
   A. Next we move on to process enhancement.
   B. But first, we need to change the pace a bit and look at two very practical issues: the law as a regulatory mechanism and forms of business ownership.

Endnotes

1. The key line from an old Wendy's commercial, featuring two older women at a rival fast food joint suspiciously eyeing their hamburger.

2. I suspect that fundamentally new and significant extensions are more commonly viewed as first mover products than are refinements.

3. This definition is based on the approach developed in Philip Kotler, *Marketing management: Analysis, planning, implementation, and control.* (9th ed.) Englewood Cliffs, NJ: Prentice-Hall, 1997, p. 605.

4. The literature on persuasive communication and its applications to marketing is extensive. If you are interested in further information, I suggest you consult with a basic marketing textbook. The Kotler text cited in Note 3 above (or newer editions) is excellent, as are many others. The classic set of experiments on persuasive communication is C. I. Hovland, A. Lumsdaine, and F. Sheffield, *Experiments in mass communication.* Princeton, NJ: Princeton University Press, 1948. For an interesting (and much more contemporary) view of how people respond to persuasive communication attempts, you may want to read M. Friestad and Peter Wright, "The persuasion knowledge model: How people cope with persuasion attempts," *Journal of Consumer Research*, June 1994, pp. 1–31.

5. "Impersonal" means that the advertisement is oriented to a class of customers, not you personally. An important recent trend is the development of targeted advertisement, which attempts to "personalize" the advertisement to the reader or viewer. For example, certain Internet technology allows advertisers to target advertisement based on the person's search patterns or buying habits.

6. A really interesting web site concerning media and media use is *www.mediapost.com*.

7. Celebrity endorsements are both big business and often controversial. At issue are such things as for what target market do they convey a positive (or negative) image (for example, please see S. Fatsis, "Can Iverson pitch to the mainstream?" the *Wall Street Journal*, June 8, 2001, pp. B1, B4) and what happens when the athlete's personal image takes a hit (please see Sam Walker and Reed Albergotti, "Woods Puts Golf Career on Hold" the *Wall Street Journal Online*, December 11, 2009, *http://online.wsj.com/article/SB126057561027788099.html?mod=djemalertNEWS*).

8. Historically, direct marketing and advertising were relatively easy to distinguish, but current technology is changing things.

9. See Kotler, *op. cit.*, p. 628.

10. You may not remember it, or ever read it, but the phrase "transaction cost" was introduced in a footnote in Chapter 2. The concept of transaction costs is vital to a well-developed model of markets and institutions (firms, governments, etc). If you are interested, there is a nice discussion that can be found in Paul Milgrom and John Roberts, *Economics, Organization, and Management*, Englewood Cliffs, NJ: Prentice-Hall, 1992, and a shorter one at *http://www.sjsu.edu/faculty/watkins/coase.htm*. The basic concept is usually attributed to Professor Ronald Coase, who won the Noble Prize for its development.

11. If all this seems really complicated, it is. The theory of market failures as an incentive to become vertically integrated was first discussed extensively by O. Williamson, *Markets and Hierarchies*, New York: Free Press, 1975. To my knowledge, the theory regarding incentives to vertically integrate is better developed than is theory about longer-term outcomes.

12. An interesting analysis involves Coca-Cola and PepsiCo by T. Muris, D. Scheffman, and P. Spiller, "Strategy and transaction costs: The organization of distribution in the carbonated soft drink industry," *Journal of Economics and Management Strategy*, 1992, *1* (1), pp. 83–128.

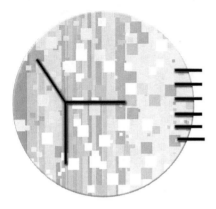

Active Practice

My strong suggestion is that you:

- Tear out the next few perforated pages from this section
- Close the book
- Answer the questions posed without looking at the book
- Please bring to class

Active Practice for Chapter 6: Linking Producers and Customers: Issues of Promotion and Channel Mix

Assume that CBA wanted to increase the number of applicants from the largest 20 cities west of the Mississippi River. Assume the budget of $50–60K per year over the next three years. Using the various elements in the promotion mix, what recommendations would you make? Please provide a brief rationale for each recommendation. How would you know whether the money was well spent?

Please go to the next page.

The overall goal of supply chain management is getting the right amount of the right stuff in the right place at the right time at the lowest possible cost.

How is achievement of this goal related to accurate demand predictions?

What are some problems if demand predictions are too high?

What are some of the problems if demand predictions are too low?

Please tear out and bring to class. Thanks.

Why All the Fuss about Productivity?

7

> *"Now, here, you see, it takes all the running you can do, to keep in the same place. If you want to get somewhere else, you must run at least twice as fast as that!"*[1]
>
> **Lewis Carroll**

I. Teaser.

   A. Imagine you are a firm in perfect competition. You want to break out. Assume that for some reason product differentiation isn't possible. What could you do?

   B. What is it that Southwest Airline has over its competition? Or Walmart?

      1. Whatever it is, it must be important. Why?

      2. First, both of these firms have been very successful in unattractive industries.

      3. Second, both of these guys entered the market <u>long after</u> very successful rivals they subsequently crushed.

      4. Third, even though each has been carefully studied by their rivals, it appears as though either the rivals can't figure out what makes them so successful <u>or</u> it's really difficult to accomplish. In practice, it's probably a bit of both.

   C. And by the end of this chapter, you should have a pretty good idea of what "it" is—it is process enhancement, particularly in the form known as productivity improvement.

II. A shift in focus: Thinking about process enhancement.

   A. Reconnect to past material.

      1. Earlier, I premised that firms attempt to avoid or escape perfect competition in their output markets. We've already discussed one route, differentiation, extensively.

      2. A second route is **process enhancement**, which involves making investments to reduce the cost of manufacture (or service creation), to increase the capabilities of the manufacturing (or service) system, or both.

   B. Basics.

      1. A <u>production system</u> is the specialized set of resources used by a firm to produce the firm's products.

         a. More common in goods production is "manufacturing system."

         b. The production system includes plant, equipment, and systems to measure and control the system (e.g., labor usage, material usage and flow, and so on). In recent years, the supply chain (<u>especially that portion linking suppliers to the firm, parts of the firm to each other, and the firm to customers</u>) has also been viewed as directly or indirectly, part of the production system.

2. Process enhancement comes in two forms:
   a. One focuses on <u>increasing the capabilities</u> of the production system.
      (1) Presumably, if the firm can develop these innovative capabilities faster (and/or better) than their rivals, they can convert this into product characteristics that provide differentiation opportunities.[2]
      (2) For example, many firms have put much effort over the past decade into improving the quality of their goods and services. Other examples include technology (1) to provide faster or new forms of distribution and (2) to have online access to ordering product or obtaining technical assistance.
   b. The second involves <u>finding ways to reduce the cost of producing</u> a good or providing a service.
      (1) This form is called productivity (or efficiency) improvement.
      (2) Presumably, if the firm can reduce the cost of production before or more rapidly than its rivals, it can reduce the price to the consumer (before or faster than its rivals), thereby gaining competitive advantage. For example, Walmart has dominated its rivals in developing ways to reduce the costs of ordering and stocking goods, and has passed much of these savings to the customer in the form of lower prices.
      (3) In general terms, we can improve productivity in two ways: making more stuff at the same total cost or making the same amount of stuff at a lower total cost (or both). <u>Either way, the average cost of the stuff goes down</u>.[3]
   c. What do we learn from the above (aside from basic definitions)?
      (1) Process enhancement may affect product characteristics directly and perhaps provide an opportunity to differentiate. Example, if the firm's production system investments improve conformance to customer specifications (relative to rivals), we may be able to differentiate of the basis of higher quality.
      (2) Process enhancement may reduce the average cost of production. I call this form of process enhancement "productivity improvement." Example, if we can reduce scrap, we should reduce material costs.
3. By the end of this set of notes, I hope to demonstrate:
   a. Productivity improvement is at least as important as product differentiation.
   b. Differentiation and process enhancement are related in that each constrains the other (i.e., it's difficult or impossible to build a production system that can achieve maximum differentiation and minimum cost simultaneously).
   c. Although both forms of enhancement are important, here we address <u>only</u> productivity and two closely related concepts, production and production rate.

C. Production, production rate, and productivity.
   1. Basic definitions:
      a. **Production (or "output" or "throughput") is the quantity produced**.
      b. **Production rate is output produced per unit time**.
      c. **Productivity is output produced per input consumed**.
   2. For example, let's examine the following data for two fictitious banks:

Weekly Data	Bank A	Bank B
# Customers served	1000	1000
# Hours open	50	40
# Tellers	2	5
# Teller hours worked★	80	200

★ Assume each teller works 8 hours a day, 5 days a week

3. Assuming no fluctuation in demand, hours, number of tellers, of teller hours worked per week, we can say that each week,
   a. <u>production</u> at Banks A and B =   1000.0   1000.0
      (units = customers)
   b. <u>production rate</u> at Banks A and B =   20.0   25.0
      (units = customers/bank-hour)
   c. <u>productivity</u> at Banks A and B =   12.5   5.0
      (units = customers per teller-hour)
   d. Please note—
      (1) <u>Production, production rate, and productivity are different.</u> Here, production rate is higher at B and productivity higher at A, even though production is identical. Many different situations exist.
      (2) If both banks pay tellers the same wage, say $10.00 per hour, then direct labor costs at Bank A are $0.80 per customer ($10.00 per hour/12.5 customers per hour), while at Bank B it's $2.00 in per customer (assuming no other direct labor costs).
4. This view of productivity is called <u>labor productivity</u>.
   a. That is, **we consider labor as the only critical input resource consumed in the production of the banking services**.
   b. Sometimes this view of productivity is useful, sometimes not.
      (1) It all depends on the firm's view of the critical input resource(s).
      (2) As we'll see, there are multiple approaches to defining productivity specific to particular industries or firms.
      (3) However, all of these various specific measures of productivity are defined as output produced per input consumed.

III. Why is productivity important?
   A. There are many, interrelated reasons, some at the level of the firm and others are at the level of the national economy.
   B. At the firm level, productivity is a measure of the efficiency by which it converts certain assets of the firm into product.
      1. In the above example, Bank A tellers are 2.5 times more productive (12.5/5.0) than those at Bank B. That is, every labor hour at Bank A produces 2.5 times as much product as a labor hour at Bank B.
      2. <u>Generally, a firm that is more productive than others in its industry is more competitive, since it needs fewer units of input to produce the same number of units of output.</u>
      3. Another way of looking at this is **all other things equal, the net income of the more productive firm is higher than the net income of the less productive firm.** This is detailed in the following example.
         a. Let's look at the two banks above in terms of a breakeven analysis. In any given week, both have the same number of customers ($Q_A = Q_B = Q$). For the moment also assume the price of each transaction is the same ($P_A = P_B = P$) and the fixed costs for both banks is the same ($F_A = F_B = F$). Then we know that:
            (1) Bank A: NI_A = PQ $- V_A Q$ $- F$
            (2) Bank B: NI_B = PQ $- V_B Q$ $- F$
         b. Subtracting (2) from (1), we have:
            (3) $NI_A - NI_B = -V_A Q + V_B Q = Q(V_B - V_A)$
         c. If we assume that the only variable costs in the Banks are the teller wages, then $V_A = \$0.80$ per customer and $V_B = \$2.00$ per customer, or
            (4) $NI_A - NI_B = \$1.20\ Q$.
         d. Hence, Bank A's NI is $1.20 more than Bank B <u>per transaction</u>.

4. Two important interim conclusions:
   a. **The first is, other things equal, the greater the productivity of the firm, the greater the net income.** This will be modified later in the discussion, but for now this is a useful conclusion.
   b. **The second is that greater productivity implies (usually) lower variable costs.**
   c. Not evident in this example, is that greater productivity may allow us to produce more units (larger Q) per unit time.
C. At the national level productivity is a measure of the relative efficiency of converting a nation's resources (inputs) into a nation's output.
   1. Generally, other things equal, "a country's ability to improve its standard of living over time depends almost entirely on its ability to raise its output per worker."[4]
   2. Although we have to be careful about drawing causal relations, the association of national level productivity and household income can be seen in Figure 7–1 (adapted from Krugman, 1991, p.11).
   3. The 1970s and 80s saw the rise in economic power of Japan and of Germany relative to the U.S. This can be observed in the relative annual growth rates of productivity in the three countries (please see Figure 7–2).
   4. Productivity growth of the U.S. economy since the mid-1990s.
      a. Sometime after about 1995, much was made of a "new economy," powered by rapid developments in technology, communication, and other fields. Many people talked of a new industrial revolution.

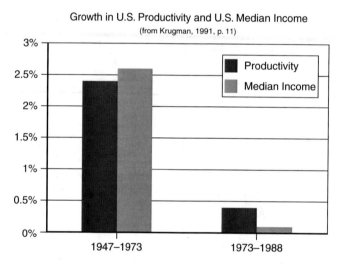

Figure 7–1

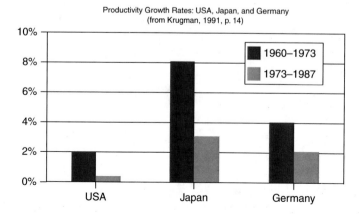

Figure 7–2

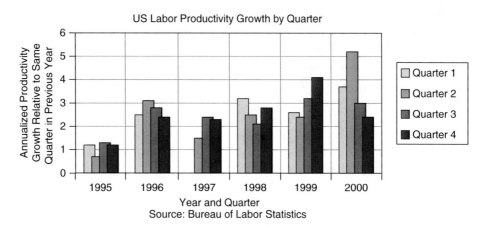

Figure 7–3

    b. One aspect of all this was an expected dramatic increase in annual productivity growth in the U.S. and perhaps worldwide.

    c. The "official data" did show some solid growth (please see Figure 7–3 above), accompanied by general increases in household income although these were concentrated in higher income brackets.

IV. Improving productivity.

    A. Given the above comments, it would seem as though improving productivity is an important goal for both nations and individual firms.

    B. Since our focus here is on the firm-level issues, we will focus only on improving firm level productivity.

       1. Let's recall: we have defined productivity as output produced per input consumed.

       2. Now, output can be measured in terms of units produced ("how many do we make?") or the value of the output ("how much is the output worth?"). Similarly, input could be in terms of units consumed (e.g., "how many labor hours?") or the cost of the input (e.g., labor cost).

       3. Not surprisingly, this produces many specific measures of productivity.

       4. Many of these are specific to particular industries or industry types:

         a. In the retail industry, a common measure of productivity is "revenue (or profit) generated per square foot of floor space," or how much revenue (or profit) is generated by each square foot of store.

         b. In the steel industry, a common measure is "tons of steel produced per labor hour" or how much steel is produced per labor hour worked.

         c. In the consulting and professional services, a common measure is "billable hours per man-week" or how many hours of service can actually be billed to clients per week that the consultant (or lawyer or whatever) works.

       5. Note that all three have the (output per unit of input) form, but each focuses on issues of particular importance to the specific industry.

    C. Given this, improving productivity concerns getting more units (or value) out per unit (or value) of input expended in the creation process. How is this done?

       1. In the basic sense, productivity increases if output increases with no increase in input, or input decreases with no decrease in output.

       2. However, more generally, productivity increases if . . .[5]

         a. the rate of increase in output > the rate of increase in input consumed, or

         b. the rate of decrease in output < the rate of decrease in input consumed.

       3. In either case, productivity increase implies lower consumption of input per unit of good produced. However, please note that (1) in the first case, productivity and production both increase, while (2) in the second case productivity increases while production actually decreases. Both cases are interesting and important.

4. OK, so the issue then turns on either increasing output (relative to input) or decreasing input (relative to output). How is this accomplished?
5. Lots of specific ways, for example:
   a. Increase the motivation or skill level of the workforce.
   b. Modify workflow to avoid unnecessary steps or procedures.
   c. Increase the speed of processing by getting faster equipment.
   d. Decreasing the amount of scrap or wasted material.
6. Notice that each of these involves some sort of expenditure.
   a. For example, improving the skill of the workforce is likely to involve investment in better or more extensive training.
   b. Usually this investment increases fixed cost, at least in the short run. The investment is risky in the sense that it is incurred before any benefits accrue and it may not result in the desired effect.
7. OK, let's put together a number of interim conclusions about productivity:
   a. All else equal, the greater the productivity, the greater the net income.
   b. Greater productivity implies (usually) lower variable costs.
   c. Usually increasing productivity involves increases in fixed costs (at least short term).
8. Combing all this yields the following central conclusion: Productivity improvements increase net income if the benefits of the improvement (in terms of a reduction in variable costs or an improvement in quantity produced per unit time or both) exceed the fixed costs of making the improvement.
9. If variable costs decrease, other things equal, contribution margin increases.[6]

D. One additional complication: Multi-factor productivity.
1. Productivity is the ratio of outputs to inputs. Obviously, there can be multiple inputs.
   a. Multi-factor productivity addresses the observation that a firm may be able to improve productivity by decreasing only a subset of these inputs, even if this may result in an increase in others.
   b. For example, one way of improving productivity is to invest in machinery that can do "the job" much faster (or better) than people. We call this "substituting capital for labor." If this substitution decreases labor units while increasing output, labor productivity will also improve.
2. This leads to complex indices of productivity, covering (usually) the simultaneous, aggregate effects of changes in various inputs (including labor, capital, energy, and intermediate goods inputs) on change in output.

E. Summarizing these ideas and integrating them with ideas in earlier parts of these notes:
1. Firms attempt to avoid or escape perfect competition in output markets via product differentiation, process enhancement, or business model change.
2. Process enhancement comes in two flavors (a) increase the capabilities of the production system (e.g., improve quality) or (b) improve productivity.
3. Process enhancement changes the production system, not the product, implying the firm continues to sell only generic product. As hinted above, and discussed below, sometimes this is not exactly true.
4. Process enhancement involves risky investment.
5. Improving productivity usually increases fixed costs (at least in the short run), and if successful, usually lowers variable cost.
6. If variable cost decreases, then (other things equal) contribution margin increases and breakeven quantity decreases. Incremental earnings may be used in many different ways:
   a. The firm could retain it in the form of higher net income.
   b. The firm could pass it on to customers in the form of lower prices.
   c. The firm could pass it to employees in the form of higher wages.
   d. The firm could invest it in additional process enhancement projects.
   e. The firm could pass it on to the community in the form of charity.
   f. The firm could pass it to owners in the form of dividends.
   g. The firm could use it to pay down debt.

7. So what does the firm actually do?
    a. Most typically, the firm does some combination of all of these.
    b. However, in highly competitive markets, especially if the product is in the mature phase of the life cycle, we more typically observe much of the benefit passing to customers in the form of lower prices.[7]
F. Please note carefully:
    1. Because productivity benefits are usually in the form of money saved rather than new product developed (as in differentiation), this benefit is remarkably flexible. In the past decade, firms have expended considerable investment to improve productivity and enhance process.[8]
    2. Is all this good for the buyer?
        a. In the short run, usually yes, as prices tend to decrease.
        b. In the long run, the picture is more mixed. If the firm is successful in dropping prices much faster than its rivals, it may force many of them out of business. If this happens, the market may shift from perfect competition to oligopoly or (in the extreme) to monopoly. If that happens, prices may start to rise as the firm diverts productivity savings from customers to internal uses or owners.
    3. Is all this good for employees?
        a. The answer is mixed: Yes, in the sense that it increases the long-term survival of the firm and may increase the long-term employment opportunity. But no, in the sense that it may reduce long-term employment opportunity because capital is often substituted for labor.
        b. Bottom line is it all depends on how the firm shares the benefits. Exactly for this reason, productivity improvement often generates heated philosophical and political debate.[9]

V. Change in focus: Linking production process and product differentiation.
    A. Think about Burger King and McDonald's for a minute.
        1. While you may prefer one to the other (or reject both), a cursory analysis suggests that both firms are rivals in the fast food industry with nearly identical product.
        2. However, if we look carefully at the two firms we notice some curious differences between McDonald's and Burger King.
        3. Please see Table 7–1 below.

Table 7–1 Comparison of McDonald's and Burger King

	McDonald's	**Burger King**
Basic Burger Product	Standardized (pre-made, pre-packaged, usually waiting for you)	Customized ("Have it your way") (assembled to order)
Burger product variations	Special case; usually involves a longer wait	Easy to accomplish
Pricing	Usually lower than BK	Usually higher than McD's
Promotion	Usually emphasizes price or quality	Usually emphasizes customized product
Production trigger	<u>Estimation of demand</u>; make to estimate; finished goods inventory	<u>Customer order</u>; make to order; Work in process (WIP) inventory
Customer flow—normal demand	Multiple queues	Usually one queue
Customer flow—high demand	Open or close queues as required by demand	Shift from one queue to two queues
Typical transaction	Order, ring-up as ordered, fill order, pay	Order, ring-up as ordered, pay, receive a receipt, fill order at a separate station

B. Are these differences by chance?

   1. Not by chance; more likely by design, at least in part.[10] How come?

   2. Back first to basics:

      a. Firms attempt to escape or avoid perfect competition.

      b. Three escape paths have been introduced, two well discussed. When introduced, we viewed the three as independent, alternative strategies.

   3. But the McD's/BK discussion suggests maybe product differentiation and productivity are not independent.

   4. Indeed, <u>not only are they not completely independent, each constrains the other</u>. To see that we introduce a new idea: the process-product matrix.

C. Product-process matrix [11]

   1. Basic idea: Investment in product differentiation has implications for productivity and investment in productivity has implications for product differentiation.

   2. Figure 7–4 presents the basic relationships.

   3. What does this mean and what's it have to do with Burger King and McD's? First we look at "what's it mean," and then we apply it to the Burger joints.

D. <u>Key point</u>: Being "on the diagonal" represents a "proper" matching of product requirements and process capabilities.

   1. This is the same thing as saying that there tends to be a "match" between differentiation strategy and process strategy.

      a. Example, if you pursue a policy of substantial product differentiation, your choice of an efficient production system is more or less constrained.

      b. Go to Figure 7–4. Locate the position on the x-axis that corresponds to "much product differentiation," trace up to the diagonal and then to the y-axis, you observe that the production process is one that is flexible, but relatively low in productivity.

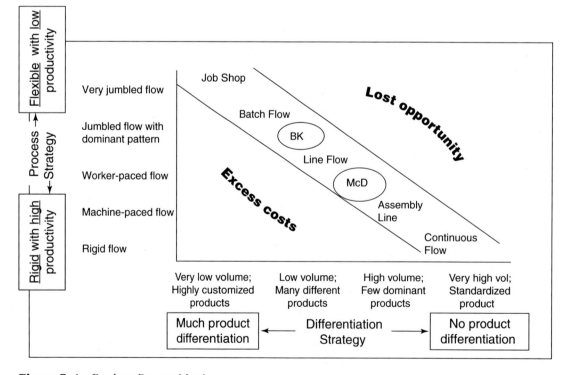

Figure 7–4   Product-Process Matrix

Adapted from Hayes and Wheelwright, "Linking Manufacturing Processes and Product Life Cycles," <u>Harvard Business Review</u>, 1979, Jan–Feb.

2. <u>This has many important implications.</u>
   a. **First**: It suggests that differentiation and process enhancement are related—in the example above, the relationship is that choice of differentiation strategy constrains process enhancement opportunities. The converse is also true: Choice of process enhancement strategy constrains differentiation opportunities.
   b. **Second**: It suggests that investment in new product development must be coordinated with investment in process.
   c. To put this in practical language, even if you can develop a cool new product, it doesn't help if your production system can't make it, or can't make it without serious interference with other products you also make.
   d. **Third**: A firm making a single product can almost always be more productive than a firm attempting to make multiple products on a single production system. (Why?)
E. Some details.
   1. There are many different kinds of production systems.
   2. In Figure 7–4, we use traditional terminology. Development in the past decade or so has modified much of this, but we need to get a feel for basics first.
   3. At one extreme, we find **job shops**. These are highly flexible production systems capable of making a huge variety of product. But, they tend to have relatively low productivity. A great example is your kitchen (or your mom's kitchen).
      a. <u>Lots of general purpose equipment.</u>
         (1) Most of these have multiple uses.
         (2) For example, the sink. You can use it to wash dishes, defrost a turkey, hold potato peelings, store dirty pots, clean the fish tank, or wash a small dog (don't tell Mom about many of these).
      b. <u>Any particular product is likely to use an idiosyncratic (or perhaps unique) set of equipment and travel an idiosyncratic (or unique) path through the equipment.</u>
         (1) Example, compare making pasta with making bacon and eggs.
         (2) This is what we mean in Figure 7–4 by the phrase "jumbled flow."
      c. <u>Much of the equipment is idle most of the time.</u>
         (1) Most kitchens are just not in use most of the time.
         (2) Even when used, much equipment is more or less idle. Some is virtually never used.
      d. The flexibility of job shops emerges from the presence of general purpose equipment that can be used in many different ways.
      e. The relatively low level of productivity occurs because much of the equipment is idle most of the time. In other words, you've made much investment in "input resource" that is often not converted into output.
      f. Job shops have another interesting problem.
         (1) Exactly because most of the equipment is not used to make any particular product, one way to increase productivity is to try to make multiple products simultaneously.
         (2) This leads to the **bottleneck problem**.
            (a) Best way to think about this is an example. When you are in Mom's kitchen making something, you have complete access to all of the equipment. But if both you and your sister are in the kitchen at the same time both making something, you tend to get in each other's way **and** sometimes you both need the same piece of equipment. As an extreme example, compare your Mom's kitchen when only you are in there versus a whole bunch of people at Thanksgiving.
            (b) <u>Bottlenecks occur when the production of one product is delayed waiting for a piece of equipment that is already in use.</u>[12]
            (c) In general, as you add products, you tend to get bottlenecks and scheduling problems. Bottlenecks and scheduling problems often adversely affect delivery commitments, costs, sometimes quality, and always productivity.

g. Volume is another problem of job shops. General purpose equipment is not designed for large volume. For example, while you can certainly bake a couple hundred cookies in Mom's oven, I doubt you can kick out thousands a day, every day. It just wasn't designed for that kind of use.

4. At the other extreme are **rigid- (or continuous-) flow systems**.

a. Assume you are making a single generic product, product demand is great, and you want to build a high-productivity production system.

b. Would you build a job shop?

   (1) Probably no.

   (2) Why?

     (a) A job shop would have flexibility you don't need (i.e., the ability to make many different kinds of product).

     (b) It wouldn't be geared to produce high volume.

c. What kind of a system <u>would</u> you build?

   (1) Probably one specifically focused on making one product, in large volume, with minimum bottlenecks.

   (2) What would such a system "look like"?

     (a) It would probably have **highly specialized equipment** focused on making only the generic product.

     (b) It would probably be constructed so that all (or most) equipment would be **used almost constantly**.

     (c) Since you have only one product, it would probably be constructed so that all products used more or less the same set of resources and follows a **standard path** through the system.

d. These are the basic characteristics of a rigid flow system.

e. Although potentially very productive, rigid flow systems also have standard problems:

   (1) **Capacity utilization**: Since we generally want to keep the equipment fully loaded more or less all of the time, demand has to be sufficient to use more or less the full capacity of the system.

   (2) **Scale**: Since these systems use specialized equipment to produce large volume, usually they involve considerable initial investment.

   (3) **Demand estimation and cyclicality**: Since (a) you wish to maintain a fully loaded system, (b) the initial investment is large, and (c) the lead-time to build the system is usually long, you have to be able to estimate future demand with reasonable precision. Moreover, seasonal and macroeconomic cyclicality or competitive action makes it very difficult to determine the correct size facility.

   (4) **Preventative maintenance**: You need to construct the system to allow systematic shut down to service the system.

   (5) **Response to technological innovation**: Since you want to maintain high productivity, you may need to upgrade the system often to take advantage of changing technology.

5. Comparing the extremes of job shops with rigid-flow systems should give you a basic feel for how production systems can vary.

a. "In between" these extremes are several other standard production systems, as noted in Figure 7–4, including batch systems, line flow, and assembly systems.

b. For the purpose of these notes, we will not go into any detail about these systems. Hopefully, you'll learn more about them in a later business courses.

c. Although the above discussion was developed from the perspective of a goods producing firm, a similar set of issues holds for a service producing firm.

6. In all this detail, it's important to recall the main point: **Differentiation strategy and process enhancement strategy are mutually constrained. Investment in one has implications for investment in the other.**

F. Applying all this to McDonald's and Burger King.
  1. OK, now let's get back to "curious" differences summarized in Table 7–1.
  2. In general, BK pursues a more differentiated product strategy than does McD's. (Please see Figure 7–4 for the "placement" of both firms on the product-process matrix.)
    a. McD's focuses on production of a standard product (you better like both mustard and ketchup), while BK views each burger as customized by the customer's order.
    b. This shows up in how BK advertises its product ("have it your way").
  3. Since we now know that differentiation and process strategy are mutually constrained, we expect to observe differences in the production systems.
    a. Technically, both firms use variants of line flow systems.
    b. But the differences, in a relative sense, are major.
      (1) The McD's system must estimate demand precisely, and then make standardized product before the customer appears so that all the counterperson needs to do is take your order and "fill from the bin."
      (2) This also informs us as to such subtle differences as a receipt at BK and not at McD's (since the order is customized you need something to check that the order received is actually what you ordered).
      (3) Since we generally observe higher productivity with systems that produce less differentiation, we may expect that the BK system is less efficient than the McD's system, producing slightly higher costs at BK. This would explain the slightly higher price at BK. Also, BK customers may expect to pay a bit more for a customized product.
  4. Please go back to Table 7–1 and try link the various differences listed to product-process issues.

VI. Summary.
  A. First, we developed the concept of process enhancement, which comes in two forms: enhancing capabilities and productivity improvement.
    1. Of these, productivity was first introduced in Chapter 2.
      a. Productivity enhancement involves risky investments that increase fixed costs (at least in the short term), hopefully reducing variable costs or increasing quantity or both in the future.
        (1) If successful, the firm may escape or avoid perfect competition by decreasing the average cost of production of a generic good, producing a competitive advantage for the firm by allowing it to pass some of these savings to the customer in the form of lower prices. Lower prices may also lead to an increase in demand for the firm.
        (2) Other things equal, higher productivity implies higher net income.
      b. Productivity may be more powerful than differentiation because the benefit can more easily address the concerns of multiple stakeholders.
    2. Second, we tried to demonstrate that product differentiation and productivity enhancement were not independent strategies, but mutually constraining.
    3. Putting these two ideas together, we observe the following:
      a. Decisions regarding the degree of differentiation a firm wishes to pursue has implications for production systems, which in turn has implications for likely levels of productivity.
      b. Generally, higher levels of productivity are possible when there is less product differentiation.
      c. Conversely, building in high levels of production differentiation usually results in a system that has lower levels of productivity.
  B. Process enhancement has evolved rapidly in the past decade or two. Hopefully, you will have a chance to see this in subsequent courses.

Endnotes

1. Lewis Carroll (Charles Litwidge Dotson), *Through the Looking Glass.*
2. Please note carefully: Until this point, we have viewed product differentiation and process enhancement as independent. As we will see later in this section, this is not strictly true.
3. It turns out things are a bit more complicated, as we'll see later in the chapter. But for now, the "two ways" approach gives you the sense. Even in the more complicated cases, the focus is reduction of the average cost of production.
4. Paul Krugman, *The Age of Diminished Expectations*, 1991, p. 9.
5. This is the complication suggested in footnote 3.
6. This implies that *one* effect of *successful* productivity improvement is that the breakeven quantity decreases. I show this graphically below. This may have the added benefit that the flexibility of the production system increases in the sense that smaller production runs may be economically feasible.

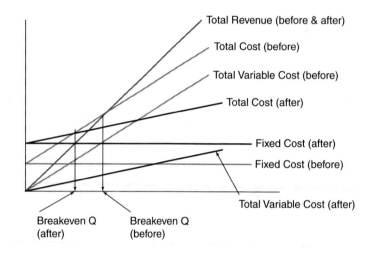

7. Please recall we demonstrated earlier in the chapter that productivity can improve even while production decreases. In the mature phase of the life cycle, often demand is slowly declining. Productivity improvements in this phase are critical, as they allow the firm to decrease its breakeven quantity to adjust to decreasing demand.
8. Please recall the "Teaser" at the start of the chapter regarding Southwest Airlines and Walmart.
9. This has been, is, and will continue to be a hot issue in the U.S. and abroad.
10. Be cautious here with the phrase "by design." What I **do not** mean to imply is that the firm can design or plan a system in a purely rational way and then plunk it in place. Rather, ideas are developed and tried, and adaptive ones are retained more often than non-adaptive ones.
11. Hayes and Wheelwright introduced the product-process matrix concept in 1979 (the reference is Hayes and Wheelwright, Linking Manufacturing Processes and Product Life Cycles, *Harvard Business Review*, 1979, Jan–Feb). Their purpose was to examine how the likely production system changes during the course of the product life cycle. My use of the concept here is a bit different, as I am less concerned here with the product life cycle and more concerned with the "match" between a firm's product differentiation strategy and its likely investment in a production process consistent with that strategy.
12. Bottlenecks can, and do, happen in all forms of production system. My point here is that they are a particular problem in job shops.

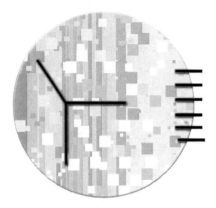

Active Practice

My strong suggestion is that you:

- Tear out the next few perforated pages from this section
- Close the book
- Answer the questions posed without looking at the book
- Please bring to class

Active Practice for Chapter 7: Why All the Fuss about Productivity?

1. What is a production system?

2. Process enhancement can occur in two forms. What are these and how do they differ?

3. Some observers believe that process enhancement provides greater opportunities for the firm than does a similar investment in product differentiation. You believe this? Why or why not?

4. In the notes I say ". . . other things equal, the greater the productivity of the firm, the greater the net income." What is the rationale behind this claim?

5. During the growth phase of the product life cycle, there is typically little incentive to the firm to invest in productivity improvement. As the firm enter the mature phase, usually there are incentives to invest in productivity improvement. What causes the shift in incentive?

Please tear out and bring to class. Thanks.

Final Comments

Well, That's It Folks

In some 160 pages, I've introduced a number of important business concepts in what I hope is a reasonably organized, internally consistent, and holistic style. My goal was not to build functional expertise, but to provide a broad framework on which to build such skill in downstream courses.

Let's briefly recall. After a two chapter overview of the most basic ideas, I introduced the conceptual spine of text, namely that firms attempt to avoid or escape perfect competition in their output markets, that three paths are available to achieve this (differentiation, process enhancement, and building new business models), and that the pursuit of any of these paths requires risky investment. This progressed to a discussion of industries and a traditional method to analyze industries. The differentiation path was developed rather extensively in Chapters 4–6 and process enhancement explicated in Chapter 7. Business model issues, please recall, were developed early (in Chapter 2).

Along the line various other topics popped up where it seemed appropriate to introduce them, and please remember that many of these are not the typical fare of "introductory" courses (for example, the interaction of market and non-market forces, stakeholder analysis, the importance of stability in markets, the critical importance of accurate demand estimation, the evolution of pull systems from both a marketing and operations perspective, a reasonably serious examination of industry analysis, a solid introduction to supply chain and operations issues, and many other topics).

While it may seem like we have covered "a lot," to be honest, all this is just step 1.

If you are using this text in conjunction with its namesake course at Pitt, you have also engaged in a major project which should have added practical substance to the "book stuff." In my opinion, business cannot be learned from a book—it also requires extensive practical experience-based learning, and to some degree that project should have helped satisfy that end (right down to the difficulty of getting teams organized and productive). Indeed, for most of the history of humans, commerce evolved without benefits of university education. My Mom was a successful entrepreneur without completing high school, and many of you have parents or grandparents who, perhaps with little formal education, started businesses sufficient to keep food on the table and maybe even grow to significant size.

So what's step 2? Honestly, I don't have a detailed answer appropriate for all. Hopefully, something in this text has grabbed you, excited you, and helped you focus your personal investment in this adventure. If so, then the advice is simply pursue that nascent dream, push your talent to its frontiers, and strive for excellence. Best wishes. Keep in touch if you want (atkin@katz.pitt.edu).